'the visions of the hills
and souls of lonely places'

———

WORDSWORTH

D.Y.CAMERON   ETCHING BY FRANCIS DODD

BILL SMITH

D. Y. CAMERON

The Visions of the Hills

ATELIER BOOKS

Edinburgh

FIRST PUBLISHED 1992 BY

ATELIER BOOKS

4 DUNDAS STREET · EDINBURGH EH3 6HZ

TEXT COPYRIGHT BILL SMITH

ISBN 1 873830 01 7

Designed and typeset by Dalrymple

Production and publishing consultant Paul Harris

Printed in Slovenia by Gorenjski Tisk

FOR AUDREY

PREFACE & ACKNOWLEDGEMENTS

SIR D. Y. CAMERON IS REMEMBERED TODAY AS A PAINTER of the Scottish landscape. His intense love for Scotland and its scenery is immediately apparent in his paintings, which capture the mystical beauty of Scotland in her various moods and seasons. However, he was much more than a landscape painter. He executed portraits and figure-subjects, townscapes and architectural studies, travelling as far afield as Egypt. In the course of a long life Cameron attained distinction as a painter and etcher, a connoisseur and collector. In the 1920s and '30s he was a man of considerable standing and influence in artistic circles on both sides of the Border. His advice on art matters was widely sought and he served on many Boards and Committees, including acting as a Trustee of both the Tate Gallery and the National Galleries of Scotland.

My interest in Cameron goes back to the early days of the Flemings' collection of Scottish art. It was started in 1968 by David Donald, a director of Robert Fleming & Co., who had a life-long interest in art. For eighteen years until his death in 1985 he applied himself with enthusiasm and flair to building up a broad collection of Scottish paintings, including a strong group of work by the Scottish Colourists. An artist he admired was D. Y. Cameron and his work featured early in the collection. I was drawn to Cameron by the fine draughtsmanship and use of delicate colour in his watercolours and the power and drama of some of his oils. I feel that he is underrated today and deserves to be more widely known. When I sought more information on him, I found that virtually nothing had been published since his death in 1945 except the catalogue of an Arts Council exhibition in 1965, marking the centenary of his birth. My subsequent research also led me to Cameron's sister Katharine. She too was an etcher as well as a watercolourist of renown. She is best known for her watercolours of flowers, but she was also an illustrator of books and a painter of landscape.

This biography would not have been possible without the kindness and assistance of a great many people. Chief among those is Rev. Robert James Gordon Watt, Cameron's great-nephew, who allowed me access to his father's typescript of the history of the entire Cameron family and whose enthusiasm, patience and help have been invaluable. Other members of the family to whom I am indebted are Professor Donald Cameron Watt, Ewen and Penny Cameron Watt and Mr. and Mrs. James Randall, who are related to Cameron's wife Jean.

I am also very grateful to Alasdair Auld, former Director of Glasgow Museums and Art Galleries, for his encouragement and help, particularly for lending me material and photographs which he collected while preparing the catalogue of the 1965 Centenary Exhibition. My thanks are also due to many in or around the Kippen area, including Mrs. Betty Dewar, James Kerr, the son of Cameron's head gardener, and Mrs. Kerr, Mr. and Mrs. Roderick Macleod, who live in Dun Eaglais, Cameron's former house at Kippen, Rev. J. Marshall Scoular, the present minister of Kippen Parish

Church, and Mrs. Scoular, Edward Younie, the son of Rev. John Younie, minister of Kippen Parish Church in Cameron's time, and the late Rev. R. W. A. Begg. Many other people have helped me with advice and inform ation, including Lady Lorna Anderson, John C. Annan and Douglas M. Annan, Dr. Mary Armour, Gilbert Bell, William Buchanan and Ian Monie of Glasgow School of Art, Susan Casteras of the Yale Center for British Art, Elizabeth Cumming, Elissa Curcio of Pittsburgh's Carnegie Museum of Art, Dr. Lindsay Errington and Ann Simpson of the National Galleries of Scotland, Jack Firth, Josephine Fitzalan-Howard, Robin Garton, Mr. and Mrs. Bill Hardie, Janet Hill of Frame & Co., Jeremy Howard of Colnaghi, David Jenkins and Susan Breakell of the Tate Gallery, John Keyworth of the Bank of England Museum, Mary Ann Lenhard of The Saint Louis Art Museum, Professor Donald Low of Stirling University, Jackie Mackenzie of the British School at Rome in London, Jill Mackenzie, Rachel Moss, Michael Pantazzi of the National Gallery of Canada, Andrew McIntosh Patrick, Joseph Sharples of the Walker Art Gallery, Liverpool, Joanna Soden of the Royal Scottish Academy, Ailsa Tanner, Dr. Angelika Wesenberg of Staatliche Museen zu Berlin, Paul Woudhuysen of the Fitzwilliam Museum, Cambridge, and Dr. Horst Zimmerman and Hans-Ulrich Lehmann of Staatliche Kunstsammlungen Dresden.

I am also indebted to the many private collectors – some of whom wish to remain anonymous – for their kindness and hospitality and, above all, their patience in allowing me to see their pictures and in having them photographed, including Mr. and Mrs. Andrew Adam, Lawrence Banks, Colin Clark, the Earl of Crawford and Balcarres, John Henderson, Sheila MacNicol, the Earl of Moray, Lady Louisa Stuart and Simon Taylor. In addition, I acknowledge the unknown owners of D. Y. Cameron's early watercolours 'A Norman Village' and 'The Citadel', which I considered had to be illustrated as fine examples of his work in this medium. I would be very interested to learn the whereabouts both of untraced works mentioned in the text and of major works (excluding Scottish landscapes and etchings) unknown to me.

I am grateful also to the curators and staff of galleries throughout Scotland and England, both public and private, who have spared the time to show me work by the Camerons in their collections, as well as the helpful staff of the Guildhall Library, the London Library, the National Art Library (Victoria and Albert Museum) and the Westminster Library in London, the National Library of Scotland in Edinburgh and the Mitchell Library in Glasgow.

Lastly, I would like to offer my thanks to Patrick Bourne for reading the manuscript and giving advice and comment, to Fiona MacAulay for assistance in listing the exhibited works of Katharine Cameron, to my colleagues in the Corporate Finance Department of Flemings for their forbearance, to my secretary Naomi Cooper for typing the various appendices, and especially to my wife Audrey, not only for the preparation of the index, but also for her patience and understanding.

BILL SMITH *July 1992*

CHAPTER ONE

CHILDREN OF THE MANSE

ON 28TH JUNE 1865 A THIRD SON WAS BORN TO MARGARET Robertson and her husband the Rev. Robert Cameron, the minister of Cambridge Street United Presbyterian Church in Glasgow. The birth must have brought joy to the parents, for their first two sons, John and Robert, had died in infancy of scarlet fever some 18 months previously, during the course of a short ministry at Egremont near Liverpool. Fortunately, a daughter Joanna, born less than a month before the deaths of the two boys, did not contract the disease.

The new arrival was baptised David Young, named after the minister of Perth's North Church for whom Robert Cameron on his ordination in 1856 had acted as assistant. Later in his life these christian names were hated by the recipient, who felt that as the eldest son he should have been given the traditional Cameron christian name of Donald. He refused to be known as David, preferring 'D. Y.', although the family continued to call him 'Davy'.[1]

D. Y. Cameron's father had been born in Paisley in 1825, the second son in a family of five sons and five daughters of John Cameron, a grocer and victualler, and his wife Mary Lawson. His paternal grandfather too was born in that town in 1789, the son of a farm servant. It is not known when their forbears moved from the clan lands of Lochaber to Paisley. By the middle of the eighteenth century Paisley had gained a considerable reputation for its weaving of fine linen and then silk and the high returns and high wages had encouraged substantial migration to the town. It is possible that the family moved down to Glasgow or Renfrewshire to work on the land in the aftermath of the Jacobite defeat at Culloden in 1746, when the clan structure was systematically destroyed, or perhaps as late as the 1770s or 1780s, when a population explosion in the Highlands, coupled with the beginning of the Clearances, forced many Highlanders to move south or to emigrate.

The family claim that John Cameron was a descendant of Dr. Archibald Cameron, a brother of 'The Gentle Lochiel', Donald Cameron of Lochiel, Chief of Clan Cameron, who joined Prince Charles Edward Stuart in the rising of 1745. Frank Rinder, for many years a close friend of D. Y. Cameron and the author of a catalogue of Cameron's etchings, mentioned this claim in the 1908 edition of the catalogue.[2] It is repeated in a somewhat sketchy profile of Katharine Cameron in her own handwriting, which she must have prepared for inclusion in an exhibition catalogue or a magazine article.[3] Archibald Cameron was a universally loved and respected doctor of medicine, who tried to dissuade the Prince from his enterprise. However, when Clan Cameron was prevailed upon to rise for the Cause, Archibald was appointed the Prince's aide-de-camp. After Culloden he helped the

Prince to evade his pursuers and eventually escaped to France with the Prince and Lochiel. Twice he returned to the Highlands on the Prince's business, but on the second visit he was betrayed and captured, taken to Edinburgh Castle and thence to the Tower of London. He was hanged at Tyburn in 1753, the last man to die for the Stuarts. Although the records are incomplete, it seems that Archibald had six sons and two daughters. However, no documentary evidence has been found either to prove or to disprove that D. Y. Cameron's great-grandfather was related to any of Archibald's sons. In his history of Clan Cameron John Stewart of Ardvorlich makes the point that many families claim descent from one or other of Archibald's sons.[4]

It seems likely that after leaving school Robert Cameron helped his father in the business. His elder brother John was destined for the ministry, but he died suddenly whilst still a student. Robert decided to assume John's mantle, matriculating at Glasgow University in 1848 at the relatively mature age of 23. He studied divinity at the universities of Glasgow, Edinburgh and Halle in Germany and was ordained in 1856. His first charge was as assistant to the Rev. David Young DD at the North United Presbyterian Church in Perth; within a few weeks Dr. Young died and Cameron took over as minister. Robert's younger brother David also was to become a minister in the United Presbyterian Church.

D. Y. Cameron's mother, Margaret Johnston Robertson[5], was born in Perth in 1839, the elder daughter of Donald Robertson, a surgeon, and his wife Jessie Hepburn.[6] Her grandfather Robert Hepburn had been a partner in a firm which was responsible for the development of the north end of Perth early in the nineteenth century, including Rose Terrace, a street of Georgian terraced houses facing the North Inch with the classical facade of Perth's Old Academy at its centre. Margaret's father died when she was eight and she lived with her mother and younger sister Catherine in Melville Street with a number of aunts. It must have been a whirlwind romance between Robert Cameron and Margaret Robertson. Margaret's home was just across the street from 31 Barossa Place, where Cameron lodged. In August 1858, barely two years after his arrival in Perth, they were married – he was 32 and she was 19. Their first child, a son John, was born in November 1859.

After four years at Perth Cameron accepted a call from a recently established United Presbyterian congregation at Egremont on the north east coast of the Wirral, just across the Mersey from Liverpool. The Camerons and their young son John moved down to adjoining Poulton cum Seacombe. A second son Robert was born in 1861 and a daughter Joanna in 1863. A few days after their daughter's birth first John and then Robert contracted scarlet fever – in less than a month the two boys were dead.

It must have been with a sense of relief mixed with intense sadness that the Camerons moved back to Scotland with their infant daughter in the second half of 1864, less than a year after the deaths of their two sons. Cameron had answered a call from Cambridge Street United Presbyterian Church in Glasgow, situated on the north east edge of the city's Commercial Centre.

PLATE I
D. Y. Cameron
T. & R. Annan & Sons Ltd

They set up home at 1 Queen's Terrace in the Woodlands district of Glasgow, a terrace of houses built in the 1850s as part of a development which incorporated the classical elevations of John Bryce's Queen's Crescent of 1840 immediately opposite. It was here that D. Y. Cameron was born, followed by Mary, known as 'Marie', at the end of 1866 and James in 1869. Thereafter the family moved to Hillhead, living first in Oakfield Terrace, where Margaret, known as 'Minnie', was born, and then at 16 Sardinia Terrace, where Katharine Cameron was born on 26th February 1874. Although she was baptised 'Catherine', she later spelt her name 'Katharine' and was known as 'Katie' to her family and friends. She signed her paintings either 'K. Cameron' or merely 'KC'. Robina, known as 'Ruby', the youngest member of the family, was born in 1878 in Hill Street in Garnethill. Around 1885 or 1886 the Camerons were on the move again, first to Bearsden for a short period, before returning to Hillhead to 10 South Park Terrace, where they lived until after Robert Cameron's death in 1898.

PLATE 2
Katharine Cameron c.1892
National Library of Scotland

The Glasgow in which the Camerons brought up their growing family presented an image of a confident, prosperous, striving city, as indeed it was. After all, in 1871 almost half of the total tonnage of ships built in Britain had been launched on the Clyde. By 1876 three quarters of Britain's merchant marine were powered by engines built in Glasgow. Locomotives built in Glasgow hauled trains on most of the railways of the world. It was no wonder that by the end of the century Glasgow could with justification consider itself not just the second city of Britain but the second city of the Empire. Glasgow and the west of Scotland had been transformed within a relatively short period into an industrial and commercial centre of world importance through the enterprise and ingenuity of merchants, industrialists and engineers. Several large industrial empires were established, generating great wealth for their owners and their families and creating an industrial elite which seemed to wield the power of life or death over those who worked for them.

However, like most cities in the grip of the second stage of the Industrial Revolution, Glasgow was a city of stark contrasts. Its population had increased at a rapid, if uneven, rate from around 84,000 in 1801 to 762,000 in 1901.[7] The pull of a large city and the hope of employment had attracted large numbers of agricultural workers displaced from the land by agricultural improvements, families from the relatively barren and over-populated Highlands and Islands, and Irish migrants. Not surprisingly, the city could not cope with this invasion and bad housing and chronic over-crowding were the inevitable lot of the poor and the helpless.

Situated on the boundary between Glasgow's Commercial Centre and Cowcaddens, Cambridge Street Church straddled the divide between rich and poor. When Cameron arrived in October 1864 its congregation numbered around 800, drawn from the relatively affluent residential districts of Blythswood and Garnethill to the west, from the crowded working class area of Cowcaddens immediately to the east, and from the industrial area around the canal basin of Port Dundas to the north. The building itself was unpretentious and did not follow the usual style of church architecture, so that both the site and the church were well suited to the mixing of rich and poor in the congregation.[8]

It would have taken Cameron some time to settle in and obtain the confidence of the congregation. As Egremont had been in marked contrast to the North Church in Perth, so Cambridge Street was very different to Egremont. Cameron's workload was now much heavier. In addition to his preaching and his various classes at the Church, he was responsible for eight Sunday schools with 80 teachers and 800 pupils, as well as supervising the Church's missions and two day schools in the poorer areas.[9] His pastoral work took him into Cowcaddens, one of the roughest areas in the city, where only a tiny proportion of the population went to church. It was densely populated and living conditions were dreadful. The pioneering Glasgow photographer Thomas Annan in his albumen prints of the courts and the dark, dank vennels of Glasgow vividly captured the overcrowded squalor and deprivation of a large section of the working class.[10] In many cases a whole family was crowded into a single room with an inadequate water supply and with little or no sanitation. Air pollution from the surrounding industries was extreme. There were frequent outbreaks of epidemics. It is no wonder that even as late as 1881 the average life expectancy of Glasgow's working class was 44 years for women and only 31 years for men.[11] At the time of Cameron's ministry the usual remedy for such conditions was strong drink – Cowcaddens' Maitland Street alone contained no less than seven licensed premises in a street of 40 houses![12]

Few details of the children's early life have survived, apart from memorable family holidays in Arran. D. Y. Cameron recalled as a child visiting his maternal grandmother and great aunts in Perth and watching The Black Watch drilling on the North Inch. On another occasion he was taken to Perth station with a group of other children to see Queen Victoria crossing from the London train to the refreshment room for breakfast.[13]

In adolescence the children had a wide circle of friends, drawn from Glasgow's large church and artistic communities. Their mother was very friendly with Mrs. Buchan, the wife of a Free Church minister and the mother of the author and statesman John Buchan. The Cameron and Buchan children also became friends, particularly Katie Cameron and Anna Buchan, who was some three years younger than Katie and was to become an author like her eldest brother, using the pseudonym 'O. Douglas'. There were many picnics and parties. Indeed Anna Buchan recalled that the most enjoyable parties she attended were at the Camerons' house.[14] In general John Buchan preferred his studies to either picnics or parties. D. Y. Cameron was to execute seven illustrations for *Scholar Gypsies*, a book of essays by John Buchan published by John Lane in 1896 when Buchan was barely 21.

Music had a special place in the life of the Camerons. For D. Y. music was a great source of enjoyment throughout his life. Both Joanna and Ruby were fine singers; Ruby also played the violin. As a boy James was a notable treble, who was in demand for oratorio; he also played the piano and married an accomplished pianist.[15] Minnie too was keen on music, being described as a student of music in the Census of 1881.

As they grew up the children played a part in the life and work of the Church. In the monthly congregational newsletter *Tidings*, started by Robert Cameron in 1887, there are frequent references to the responsibilities they each carried out.[16] Joanna, Marie, James and Katie were teachers in one or other of the Sunday Schools. D. Y. and James were active at Gospel Temperance meetings '... having charge of the entertainments'. At one time or another D. Y. was a teacher in the Church's Mission School in Sawmillfield Street, President of the Church's branch of the Glasgow Young Men's Christian Association, and the President or a Director of the Juvenile Missionary Association. Minnie was a Collector for the Missionary Association. D. Y.'s involvement with the Church's Music Committee and the Sunday School extended beyond his marriage in 1896 – he resigned as Superintendent of the congregational Sunday School only in 1898, when his wife and he moved to London for a short period.

The family's dedication to the Church continued into adulthood. James went on to become a minister and Marie, Minnie and Ruby married ministers. Although D. Y. did not study for the ministry, as his father might have wanted, the Church was to be a central element in his life right up to the day he died. Joanna, the only one of the children not to marry, did social work for the Church and other charitable bodies, particularly the YWCA. Along with James she served with the Scottish Churches Huts in France during the First World War – James never recovered completely from his experiences of the bombing, the memories haunting him throughout his life.[17] In recognition of her work Joanna was one of the first recipients of an OBE.

The Camerons were a very close family. D. Y. was three and a half years old when James was born and as boys they were inseparable. In a letter after James's death in 1938 D. Y. wrote:

'... he was my oldest companion and in early days we did everything together. I shall for ever miss him and the riches of his mind and imagination'.[18]

Until his marriage in 1896 D. Y. was also very close to Katie, who hero-worshipped the brother almost nine years her senior. Katie wrote in the back of a notebook in 1930:

'I remember always his great love for me and mine for him. There was no one in my childhood days like Davy. He was my hero and I adored him. When he went to study in Edinburgh at the Academy Schools, he used sometimes to come home for the weekends. I was his inseparable companion ... After his marriage this dear comradeship was ended, to my grief, never more to be regained. His wife did not understand, having had no brothers of her own, the relationship of an elder brother for a small sister'.[19]

With only four years between them Katie and Ruby too were devoted to each other in their youth. They were to remain great companions throughout their lives.

1 Attached to a letter dated 28th October 1924 from Cameron to Sir Evelyn Shaw at the London office of the British School at Rome is a small slip: 'Never, Never, Never, David, please only D. Y. The former makes me depressed and effeminate'.
2 Frank Rinder, *Etchings of D. Y. Cameron*, Otto Schulze & Company, Edinburgh, 1908, p.viii
3 NLS ACC 8950.32
4 John Stewart, *The Camerons: a History of Clan Cameron*, 1974, p.228
5 Margaret's middle name is variously spelt 'Johnston', 'Johnstone' and 'Johnson'
6 She was also known as 'Janet'
7 Andrew Gibb, *Glasgow: the Making of a City*, London, 1983, pp.105, 124
8 James Brown, *Life of John Eadie, DD LLD*, London, 1878
9 Ibid.
10 Anita Ventura Mozley, *Thomas Annan: Photographs of the Old Closes and Streets of Glasgow 1868-1877*, New York, 1977
11 Simon Berry & Hamish Whyte (eds), *Glasgow Observed*, 1987, p.145
12 Ibid., p.119
13 *Perthshire Advertiser*, 7th November 1942
14 O. Douglas, *Unforgettable, Unforgotten*, London, 1945, p.85
15 Watt
16 Cambridge Street Church Records, Mitchell Library, Glasgow
17 Watt
18 Ibid.
19 Ibid.

CHAPTER TWO

STUDENT DAYS

D. Y. CAMERON AND HIS SISTER KATHARINE INHERITED their artistic abilities from their mother, who was a talented amateur water-colourist. There is no record that she ever exhibited her work, but in 1983 five small floral studies and two larger still lifes of fruit were sold at auction by the family along with a large number of watercolours and prints by both D. Y. and Katharine.[1]

D. Y. Cameron's interest in art was awakened early in his education at Glasgow Academy. He entered the old school in Elmbank Street in Glasgow's Commercial Centre in 1874, when he was nine years old. He enjoyed his time at school, describing it in an article which he contributed to a book commemorating the centenary of Glasgow Academy as '… a beautiful chapter of early life'.[2] Writing at the age of 80 during the last year of his life, he went on:

'My recollection of the masters is vivid, and I admired and respected all, much more than they could respect me, as, after quite a good beginning, I fell in love with Art, and books and lessons were neglected. This turning aside to the left, instead of the right, was largely because of the influence of a memorable figure,

PLATE 3
Hills of Ross c.1934
Oil on panel, 6 x 9
Flemings

Mr. John Maclaren, the Writing master, who, in the old Academy days, invited perhaps a dozen boys, in whom he was interested, to remain after school hours, to receive from him special instruction in drawing. His enthusiasm and help were of infinite value, and this precious extra hour was looked forward to as the golden moment of the day.

'I owe much to his influence and friendship in after years, when, in the new Academy[3], he organised and led his famous choir, thus turning many to the deepest and most beautiful elements within us.

'A second figure, never-to-be-forgotten, was Dr. James Colville, head of the English Department, whose grace and teaching went far beyond facts to love of great poetry and beauty of language. The memory of these two men remains as something by itself in life, and enjoyed in these early and impressionable years, never fades'.

In the same article he remembers:

'... many boys who won the prizes and medals, admired and cheered by masters and friends as the coming conquerors of the world – but those who followed the Arts won no applause, and were greeted on one occasion I remember with the remark, "Fingers, Fingers"'.

John Maclaren – nicknamed 'Bulldog' Maclaren because he was a stickler for discipline – joined the staff of Glasgow Academy from Hamilton Place Academy in Edinburgh in 1862, serving the school for 45 years. Both he and his wife were very keen on music and in 1878 Maclaren formed the Glasgow Academy Choir – its annual concerts in the former Queen's Rooms were considered a great social event. In the 1890s Cameron etched covers for two concert programmes.[4]

While still in his final year at school Cameron commenced classes at Glasgow School of Art. At that time Charles Rennie Mackintosh's master-work in Renfrew Street was almost 20 years in the future and the School occupied somewhat cramped premises overlooking Sauchiehall Street and Rose Street in a block of buildings which included Glasgow's Corporation Galleries of Art. Robert Greenlees was in his final year as Director and Head Master. As well as day classes, the School offered early morning classes from 7am to 9am on Tuesdays to Fridays and evening classes from 7pm to 9pm from Mondays to Thursdays, making a long day for the budding artist. Apart from a mention in the School's Annual Report that he won a £1 Haldane Prize for 'Geometry' in his first year, it is unknown which classes Cameron attended. Sir James Caw, the author of *Scottish Painting Past and Present*, noted that he had 'early training as an architect'.[5] There is no mention in the family papers of any intention to become an architect, but it may be that Cameron attended classes in architecture while at Glasgow School of Art. However, he was to develop a wonderful facility for depicting architectural subjects.

Cameron left Glasgow Academy in 1881, when he was 16. Through a leading member of his father's congregation he obtained a position in the office of a Glasgow iron foundry.[6] This must have been something of a compromise. Certainly it was against the wishes of his father, who may have wanted his son to remain at school and then follow the family tradition of studying for the ministry.[7] Cameron hated office work, but he stuck at it, continuing with his studies at Glasgow School of Art, where he was mentioned in the Annual Reports for 1881–82 and 1883–84 as receiving prizes or commendations in a number of the classes. After two years or so he left Glasgow for his mother's home town of Perth and spent a short, but equally unhappy, period working in the law office of his great-uncle David Hepburn, who at the age of 87 was still in practice.

Sometime in 1884 Cameron finally came to the conclusion that he could not go on as he was doing, but had to become a painter. Not surprisingly, his father's response was cool – in that case, he would have to fend for himself.[8] He decided to go to Edinburgh and enrol for art classes there. He may have been encouraged in this idea by William Miller Frazer (1864-1961), who was born and bred in Perth and was about the same age as Cameron. It seems likely that the two artists met during Cameron's stay in Perth and Frazer would have told him that shortly he was going to Edinburgh to study art. Certainly the two studied together in Edinburgh and became life-long friends.

Art classes in Edinburgh were organised by two national bodies, which at best tolerated each other's existence and on occasions carried on acrimonious disputes, usually related to competing claims on accommodation. Formal classes covering a number of disciplines were provided at the Trustees' Academy, located in the Royal Institution building fronting

PLATE 4
Stirling Castle from Raploch 1904
Watercolour over pencil, 13½ × 18½
Glasgow Art Gallery & Museum

Princes Street at the Mound. Established as a school of design in 1760, the Trustees' Academy during the greater part of the nineteenth century trained most of those artists who were later to become members of the other body – the Royal Scottish Academy. The latter organised a Life Class in the building which it shared with the National Gallery situated on the Mound behind the Royal Institution. By the 1880s the standard of art training had deteriorated from that achieved a quarter of a century earlier, when the Trustees' Academy under its inspiring Director Robert Scott Lauder had turned out artists such as George Paul Chalmers (1833-78), William Quiller Orchardson (1832-1910), John Pettie (1839-93) and William McTaggart (1835-1910).[9] The RSA's Life Class too was in poor shape, meeting in cramped accommodation – 'a tunnel, a railway tunnel' – and supervised by a Curator, the fine anatomical draughtsman George Clark Stanton (1832-1894), and four Academician Visitors rather than appointed teachers.[10] However, it was still a very good forum for students to meet each other and exchange ideas and experiences.

It is unclear whether Cameron attended classes at the Trustees' Academy or the RSA's Life Class or both. Sir James Caw and Frank Rinder, both of whom became close friends of Cameron, record that he attended the RSA Life Class. This is repeated in the notice of Cameron's death in the RSA Annual Report for 1945. Yet his signature does not appear in the Registers of Attendees maintained by the RSA.[11]

In Edinburgh, freed from the numbing drudgery of office routine, Cameron could concentrate full-time on his art, immersing himself in the shared excitments and adversities of life as an art student. As well as Frazer, fellow students at that time included George Denholm Armour (1864-1949), Charles Mackie (1862-1920), James Pryde (1866-1941) and William Walls (1860-1942). He joined the Scottish Atelier Society; Arthur Melville was one of the artist-visitors who helped students with advice and comment on their work.[12] One of the most exciting events during his time in the city must have been the Edinburgh International Exhibition held in 1886. Featured in its fine art section was a strong group of French and Dutch paintings lent by British collectors. There were 192 works in all, including 22 by the Hague School painter Matthijs Maris (1839-1917), who was to exert a considerable influence on Cameron's early work.

In 1886 Cameron exhibited his work for the first time. At the RSA's annual exhibition that year he showed two oil paintings – 'Early Morning in a Highland Valley' (£20) and 'The Convent Minstrel' (£15). The same year he exhibited a sketch 'Jacobites' (£5) at the Glasgow Institute of the Fine Arts, the rival exhibiting society in Glasgow. There is no record of whether he managed to sell his work!

All-in-all it was an exhilarating period for Cameron. In a letter written in 1941, enclosing a sketch of Cameron which Frazer had executed in Cameron's lodgings in Edinburgh in November, 1884, Frazer recalled their days there:

> 'Duncan, Walls and ourselves are the only lot left of that time ... I can never forget your quenchless enthusiasm for work and your adoration of Paul Chalmers, Pettie and Orchardson'.[13]

Orchardson, who had moved to London in 1862 and was elected a Royal Academician in 1877, was very highly regarded both by his contemporaries and by the following generation of art students. In the latter it amounted almost to hero-worship. Cameron later recalled how he and a group of fellow students travelled from Glasgow to Edinburgh on the evening of an RSA banquet merely to get a glimpse of Orchardson as he got out of his cab and entered the RSA.[14]

How he managed to live during his time in Edinburgh can only be guessed. Presumably he tried to sell some of his sketches and he would have taken what jobs he could, perhaps as an illustrator for papers and periodicals. His sister Katharine recalled that he went home to Glasgow at many weekends.[15]

Cameron returned to Glasgow during 1887. He was then 22 years of age, a strong, squarish man of under medium height, clean shaven with blonde hair, blue eyes, 'a straight bridged nose and a biggish but smiling mouth'. He did not look like an artist. Throughout his life he was careful about his appearance; he was always neatly dressed. He abhorred slovenliness in anything. His upbringing as a son of the manse was reflected in his preference for dark clothes. He resolutely refused to wear the kilt, prompting a sister to exclaim 'And him a Cameron too!'[16, 17]

The same year a chance encounter was to have a profound bearing on the direction he was to take as an artist. A couple of sketches he had placed in a shop window hoping for a sale were seen by George Stevenson, the brother of Daniel Macaulay Stevenson, the Glasgow industrialist and future Lord Provost, and the artist Robert Macaulay Stevenson, one of the Glasgow Boys. After Cameron's death Nancy Reece, a relative or friend of

George Stevenson, described what followed:

'... it was the merest chance that George Stevenson discovered him. I was riding home with Mr. Stevenson and something went loose in my stirrup. He got down to see to it in a mean little street off the [Great] Western Road. In a small shop window he caught sight of two pen and ink sketches marked 3/6 and was so struck with them that he helped me off my horse to go and look at them. We went in and bought them, and we asked for the address of the artist, which the shopkeeper refused to give. However, Mr. Stevenson was so struck by the talent shown in the little sketches that he determined to find the artist, and after some trouble he succeeded in doing so. Himself a Fellow of the Painter-Etchers Society and a great enthusiast, he invited D. Y. Cameron to our house, and at once began to teach him everything about etching, from the first sketch to the finished print, which was all done in our house. He felt quite sure about D. Y. Cameron's talent, and persuaded him, with great difficulty, to become seriously an etcher by profession. At that time D. Y. Cameron was teaching in some school, whether all the time or only in the evening I cannot remember, but he was very much afraid to give up his regular salary for the precarious 'life of an artist'. However, Mr. Stevenson financed him, introducing him to reliable dealers, and publishing his first series of Clyde etchings'.[18]

There is no mention in the family papers of Cameron teaching in a school on his return to Glasgow in 1887. It is possible that he may have accepted a part-time post as an art teacher at a private school or acted as a teacher for evening classes organised by the Glasgow School Board. Nancy Reece was writing some 58 years after the event and it may be that some of the details had become rather hazy in her mind. However, there can be no doubt about the principal facts, which also were documented by Frank Rinder.[19]

Stevenson was about seven years older than Cameron and a partner in his brother Daniel's firm of D. M. Stevenson & Co., Glasgow shipowners and coal and iron exporters. He was an enthusiastic amateur etcher, a friend of the noted etcher Sir Francis Seymour Haden, who was the brother-in-law of Whistler and had been the moving force behind the creation of the Society of Painter-Etchers in 1880. Stevenson himself was a Fellow of the Society from 1881 to 1888 and exhibited at a number of the Society's exhibitions. It was in Stevenson's home at 322 St. Vincent Street that Cameron was able to study at first hand fine prints from Stevenson's own collection and was introduced to the techniques of etching. Cameron was to become one of the foremost British etchers of his age. His later prints were avidly sought by collectors worldwide during that remarkable etching revival which lasted for almost 50 years until serious collecting was killed off by the Wall Street Crash of 1929 and the Depression.

[1] Phillips, Edinburgh, 15th July 1983
[2] The Glasgow Academy 1846-1946, Glasgow, 1946
[3] Glasgow Academy moved to its present site at Kelvinbridge at the end of 1878.
[4] Rinder (R.192, R.268)
[5] Sir James Caw, Scottish Painting Past and Present 1620-1908, Edinburgh, 1908, p.458 (Caw omitted the point when he wrote the article below)
[6] Sir James Caw, Old Watercolour Society Club Vol. 27, 1949, p.2 (the name of the iron foundry is not known)
[7] Rinder
[8] Sir James Caw, Old Watercolour Society Club Vol. 27, 1949, p.2
[9] Esme Gordon, The Royal Scottish Academy 1826-1976, Edinburgh, 1976, p.161
[10] Ibid. , p.153
[11] RSA Library, Edinburgh
[12] Rinder, p.xxxii (information about the Society is scant – its name suggests that it may have been an informal association of young artists, meeting regularly in a particular studio, perhaps hiring a model for life study, and having established artists as occasional 'visitors' to offer advice and comment; the Society had folded before 1908)
[13] NLS ACC 8950.1 (the identity of the Duncan referred to in the letter is difficult to establish with any certainty. It could be David Duncan (1869-1943), who studied in Edinburgh and became chief damask designer at the Victoria Linen Works in Dunfermline, or the artist John Duncan (1866-1945), who was a friend of both D. Y. and Katharine Cameron, but he did not train in Edinburgh and did not move there from Dundee until around 1892)
[14] Stanley Cursiter, Scottish Art, London, 1949, p.121
[15] Watt
[16] Sir James Caw, Old Watercolour Society Club Vol. 27, 1949, p.5
[17] Florence Robertson Cameron, 'The Gospel of D. Y. Cameron: A Personal Memory', The British Weekly, 8th July 1965 (Florence Cameron was D. Y. Cameron's sister-in-law – the wife of his brother James)
[18] Letter published in Glasgow Herald on 5th October 1945 (the relationship of Nancy Reece to Stevenson is not known – she was not his wife as was reported in the Glasgow Herald a few days later)
[19] Rinder, p.xxxii

CHAPTER THREE

'GLESCA'

D. Y. CAMERON LAUNCHED HIS CAREER AS AN ARTIST AT A
particularly exciting time in Glasgow's history. It was no coincidence that
there was a remarkable flowering of painting and the decorative arts as the
city approached the peak of its industrial and commercial prosperity around
the turn of the century. This culminated in a fusion of industry and the arts
in Glasgow's International Exhibitions held in 1888 and 1901.

Glasgow had come a long way from the cultural desert encountered by
Joseph Farington, when he visited the city in 1801. Farington, a landscape
artist and Royal Academician who is remembered today more for his *Diary*
than his painting, was told:

> '... the minds of the inhabitants, including the most opulent, are not in any
> degree disposed to look to the fine arts. Trade and good living occupy their
> thoughts, and another generation must arise before any encouragement of
> painting, etc. can be expected.'[1]

The prediction was remarkably accurate. As Glasgow prospered and mat-
ured, so too did the arts. There was an ever increasing awareness of art and
the pleasures to be derived from looking at it – and owning it.

The public's interest in art had been stimulated by Glasgow's growing
civic collection, the nucleus of which came from Archibald McLellan, a
wealthy Glasgow coachbuilder and friend of Sir David Wilkie. When
McLellan died in 1854 he bequeathed to the city not only his fine collection
of Old Masters, but also the galleries in Sauchiehall Street which he was
having built to house his pictures. Painting received further encouragement
in 1861 when the Glasgow Institute of the Fine Arts was established by a
group of prominent citizens, including a number of artists. Their aims were
to foster art and provide a showcase for Glasgow and west of Scotland
artists to exhibit their work, which they claimed was denied to them by the
parochial attitude of the RSA in Edinburgh. The first exhibition attracted
39,099 visitors, a large proportion of whom had purchased 'Working Men's
Tickets'.[2] In addition to work by local artists the Institute included in its
annual exhibitions paintings by foreign artists, such as Corot and the
Barbizon and Hague School painters, as well as English artists like Burne-
Jones, Leighton, Millais, Rossetti, Watts and Whistler, thus expanding the
horizons of Glasgow's artists and public alike. The artists themselves formed
Glasgow Art Club in 1867. Whereas anyone could join the Institute,
membership of Glasgow Art Club was by election only and was tightly
controlled by Glasgow's art establishment.

The wealth generated by Glasgow's commercial and industrial success
created a growing number of art collectors. By the 1870s purchases of art
by Glasgow business men and industrialists had reached sizeable

PLATE 6
The Three Gables c.1923
Oil on canvas, 23⅝ × 15¾
Private Collection

proportions. Profits from sales at the Institute's exhibitions were so good that it could afford to build its own rather grand galleries in Sauchiehall Street, which were opened in 1879. This increased interest in art, together with greater discernment on the part of a number of collectors, who were no longer content to buy somewhat meretricious paintings at the Institute, but wanted advice on the work of Scottish and foreign artists, led to the establishment in Glasgow of a number of art dealers.

One of the first was Craibe Angus, who opened a gallery in 1874. He had good connections with Holland – his daughter Isabella later married the art dealer E. J. van Wisselingh, whose father Hendrik had been a dealer in Amsterdam. Thus Angus was well placed to deal in Hague School paintings, which proved very popular with Scottish collectors.[3] Indeed, by 1878 Glasgow collectors had acquired from Angus or other sources at least twelve works by Jozef Israels, three by both Jacob Maris and his brother Willem Maris and four by Alexander Mollinger.[4] A decade later four Glasgow collectors alone could lend from their collections no fewer than 18 of the 63 works by Hague School artists which were exhibited at the Glasgow International Exhibition in Kelvingrove Park in 1888.[5] This exhibition, the first of four great exhibitions of industry, science and art to be mounted by Glasgow over the following 50 years, had a strong fine art section, which must have been subjected to intense critical study by D. Y. Cameron and his fellow artists. Many of them submitted works for sale – Cameron himself exhibited two pairs of sketches priced at five guineas a pair.[6]

The most notable of Glasgow's art dealers was Alexander Reid, who began dealing in a small way in 1877, whilst employed in his father's firm of Kay and Reid, carvers and gilders.[7] After a short period in Paris with the renowned art dealers Boussod & Valadon, when he worked alongside Theo van Gogh and met his brother Vincent, who painted two portraits of him, Reid opened his own gallery in Glasgow in 1889 – La Societe des Beaux-Arts.[8] He was the first dealer to show the work of the Impressionists in

PLATE 7
The Waning Light 1905
Watercolour, 21¼ x 30¼
National Gallery of Scotland

Scotland and to handle Whistler's paintings. Reid was to become one of the foremost art dealers in Britain, dealing well into the third decade of the twentieth century in the work of the Impressionists and Post-Impressionists as well as Scottish painters like the Glasgow Boys and the Scottish Colourists. Sir William Burrell, one of Reid's best known clients, wrote of him:

'He did more than any other man has ever done to introduce fine pictures to Scotland and to create a love of art.'[9]

However, it was not only the monied classes who were interested in art. As has been noted, the man in the street visited the civic art collection and the exhibitions in the Institute in increasing numbers. In an article in the *Glasgow Art Review* in 1946 William Power recalled his childhood days in Glasgow, when the work of the 'Glasgow Boys' was being shown at the annual exhibitions of the Glasgow Institute of the Fine Arts:

'I was too young to be fully conscious of what was going on, but I was caught up by the enthusiasm of my older associates, all ordinary folk. The crowded Institute was as exciting as cup-tie football. Arguments were raging in front of every 'Glasgow' canvas, and they were continued at home over the tea-cups.'[10]

The Glasgow Boys were a group of young artists sharing common ideals about painting, who came together in Glasgow in the early 1880s. They did not all live in Glasgow, but at various times used or visited studios in that city. For a brief period they challenged the art establishment and revitalised Scottish art. However, their reputation was made in Europe and North America, rather than in Glasgow. Ironically, history was to repeat itself some ten years later, when Charles Rennie Mackintosh and the Glasgow Style, Glasgow's own version of Art Nouveau, received much the same treatment.

The Boys were a loose-knit band of artists, who painted in small groups: W. Y. Macgregor and James Paterson; James Guthrie, E. A. Walton, Joseph Crawhall and George Henry. John Lavery, William Kennedy, Alexander Roche and Thomas Millie Dow met in France, either while studying in Paris or while painting at Grez-sur-Loing, an old village to the south of Paris which in the 1870s and 1880s became a focus for a number of Scottish, English, Irish and American artists. For several years from about 1881 many of the Boys congregated in the winter at Macgregor's studio at 134 Bath Street for life classes and discussion. The studio became the nearest to a Paris atelier to be found in Scotland. The Boys were to travel widely, painting at various locations in Scotland, including Cockburnspath – Scotland's Barbizon – and Galloway, in Lincolnshire in England, and in France, Spain, North Africa, the Middle East and Japan.

They were united in their rejection of the academic values of the art establishment, whether exemplified by the established, but now largely forgotten, Glasgow painters such as Alexander Davidson and Duncan MacKellar, who ruled Glasgow Art Club, or by the staid, blinkered attitudes of a majority of the Academicians of the RSA in Edinburgh, led by a reactionary and often rashly outspoken President, Sir William Fettes

PLATE 8
Stirling Castle c.1898
Watercolour over pencil, 7¾ × 9¾
Flemings

Douglas. They despised the highly finished romantic landscapes and sentimental and anecdotal figure paintings of the 'Gluepots', the term of derision that they used to describe the establishment men. Turning away from the nineteenth century tradition of Scottish painting, they espoused the ideals of the young French painter Jules Bastien-Lepage (1848-1884) and the Barbizon and Hague School artists. Adopting a style characterised by a vigorous handling of paint and a bold use of colour, the Boys set out to emulate Bastien-Lepage's 'naturalist' painting, depicting the day-to-day life of his home village of Damvillers.

Towards the end of the 1880s the Boys' early realism gave way to a decorative phase, influenced by one of the Boys themselves, Arthur Melville, by Monticelli, twelve of whose paintings had been exhibited at the Edinburgh International Exhibition of 1886, and by the Japanese print. This decorative treatment, which included a symbolist element, is seen at its strongest in the work of the younger Boys, notably George Henry and E. A. Hornel, as well as in the early work of David Gauld and the flower pieces of Stuart Park.

The critics were slow to appreciate the worth of the Boys. It was not until eighteen works by fourteen of their number had been hung at the final exhibition of the Grosvenor Gallery in London in 1890, a gallery which had a reputation for showing work by the more avant-garde artists, that the critics and the public took much notice of them. The description 'Glasgow School' was used for the first time by the critic of *The Saturday Review*. Adolphus Paulus of the Munich Art Society visited the exhibition and was so impressed that he invited the Boys to exhibit as a group in Munich's Glaspalast that year – seventeen of them showed 60 works.[11] They were an outstanding success.

D. Y. Cameron has often been identified as one of the Boys – in the 1890s the critics described him as a Glasgow Boy and David Martin included him in his book *The Glasgow School of Painting* published in 1897 (but he omitted Arthur Melville!). However, Cameron was about eight years younger than the average age of the Boys and he did not return to Glasgow from Edinburgh until 1887. Consequently, he did not associate with the Boys in their formative years. Even on his return a good proportion of his time and energy was taken up with etching. Probably it was not until after his election to Glasgow Art Club in 1891 that he associated with them, and even then he was never more than on the periphery. He did not exhibit with the Boys at the Grosvenor Gallery or in Munich in 1890. However, he did show at the New English Art Club with Macgregor, Paterson and Roche in 1892 and again in 1893 with Macgregor and Roche. He joined the Boys in the inaugural exhibition at the Grafton Gallery in London in 1893 and he exhibited with Guthrie and Lavery at the Salon, Champ de Mars in Paris in 1895. The same year he was invited to exhibit with the Boys in America at St. Louis, but, as the compiler of the catalogue noted, Henry, Park and he '... it is much regretted, had no works on hand ...'.[12]

However, it was as an etcher, rather than as a painter, that Cameron first came to prominence in the early 1890s. Initiated into the mysteries of etching by George Stevenson in 1887, he immediately threw himself wholeheartedly into his work. Almost from the outset he also experimented with drypoint. Etching involves the artist drawing with a needle on a metal plate, usually copper, coated with a thin layer of melted waxes, gums and resins. Acid is then used to bite lines in the plate where the needle has exposed the metal, the length of time the plate is left in the acid determining the depth and breadth of the bitten line. Drypoint involves drawing with a needle directly on a polished metal plate. The action of the needle on the plate produces a 'burr', which gives the line a rich velvety texture when inked. Very often etching is combined with drypoint. Until 1898 the vast majority of Cameron's plates were etched. From 1899 etching and drypoint or etching touched with drypoint was the norm. After 1910 most of his Scottish landscapes were executed in drypoint. Cameron was very particular about the quality of the printing. Apart from the early 'sets' of etchings, he invariably did the printing himself, thus ensuring the exact tones which he wished to achieve by careful regulation of the amount of ink on the plate. He had no hesitation in rejecting impressions with which he was not satisfied – in 1899 he wrote to his agent James Connell:

> 'Your telegram received & you will have the ten 'Crucifix's' on Monday morning. Some of my proofs were not good enough & I am printing finer ones at Goulding's.'[13]

In addition to using the traditional Japanese paper, he scoured bookshops at home and on the Continent for supplies of antique paper. In most cases he pulled only a few impressions from his early plates as and when he could sell them. Even after 1900, when the demand for his prints was assured, he printed in small editions, averaging only around 50 impressions each, always anxious that the quality of the print should not deteriorate through over-use of the plate. He was opposed to the practice of steel-facing a plate in order to increase the number of prints pulled, because he considered that it affected the quality of the image, writing to a dealer who had enquired about the availability of certain prints:

> 'I regret you have not been able to secure proofs of these last dry-points, and that I can do nothing to help you. The editions were so small that many who have collected my work for years could not secure them. This is one of the difficulties in collecting, but there is no way to avoid it, plates will only yield a limited edition without steel-facing, and this I never do'.[14]

Being a 'canny' Scot where money was concerned, his prices reflected the number of impressions available:

> 'Herewith a proof of 'Roslin' ... I raised the price to £4. 4. – when I saw the plate would only stand a small edition. . .'[15]

Cameron's output was prodigious – over the 13 years up to 1900 he executed 231 etchings, as well as 50 illustrations and a number of book plates. In all he produced some 520 plates – mainly architectural subjects and landscapes – in a career which spanned 45 years and lasted until 1932, when finally he gave up etching. A considerable number of the early plates were drawn with the needle from life, but the majority were executed in his studio either from drawings or, later, relying on notes and his remarkable memory. Cameron was much more interested in getting the composition right than in fidelity of detail. In both his etching and his painting he treated his subject freely, changing or omitting details or even features of a building or a landscape to suit his compositional idea.

However, it is fair to say that Cameron did not display the immediate brilliance which characterised the work of his two younger Scottish contemporaries, Muirhead Bone (1876-1953) and James McBey (1883-1959). Progress was relatively slow and it took a number of years of steady development for him to reach a position of mastery in terms of technique and composition. As a student he had executed a number of sketches of Scottish scenes in pencil and pen and ink in a style similar to that of Sir George Reid (1841-1913), the distinguished portrait painter and President of the RSA from 1891 to 1902, who was also a fine landscape draughtsman in pen and ink. It is possible that in the capacity of an Artist Visitor Reid may have given help and guidance to the young Cameron during his studies in Edinburgh, which coincided with Reid's move to that city from Aberdeen. Cameron's early etchings were of a similar nature to his sketches. His first attempts were of scenes in and around Paisley – the 'Paisley Set' of seven etchings, which were printed in London and published by Matthew Neilson of Paisley – and an atmospheric depiction of Linlithgow Palace at night (R.8), which gives the merest hint of things to come.

In 1888 he etched 21 plates, depicting scenes of Glasgow and the Clyde, Arran, Perthshire and the Borders. No doubt prompted by George Stevenson, he submitted one of these prints – 'A Perthshire Village' (R.20), thought to be near Bridge of Earn – to the Council of the Society of Painter-Etchers in London, on the strength of which he was elected an Associate of the Society on 20th February, 1889 at the age of 23.

The 'Clyde Set' followed in 1889 – twenty etchings of scenes of the River and Firth of Clyde. 22 complete sets were printed in London by Goulding, the foremost printer of etchings in the country, signed by Cameron and published by George Stevenson.[16] The same year Cameron exhibited for the first time at the annual exhibition of the RE, showing five of his etchings executed the previous year, including 'A Perthshire Village', each offered for sale at a price of twenty-five shillings framed or one guinea unframed. He was to exhibit each year until his resignation in 1903, showing a total of 122 plates and becoming one of the mainstays of the RE.

The Clyde Set brought him to the notice of James Connell, the Glasgow art dealer, who commissioned an etching of 'The Old Revenge' (R.50), then an Industrial Training Ship moored in the Gareloch. It was one of the largest plates etched by Cameron, for which he was paid £30, and was published by Connells in 1890 in an issue of 100, each signed by the artist.[17] Cameron was grateful for the commission and reminded Connell of it in 1897:

'As promised I enclose you a list of the etchings left today with prices. I am very glad indeed to have renewed business with you and do not forget that you

PLATE 9
The Steps *1892*
Etching, 10 × 3
Garton & Co

gave me my first impartial commission which at that time was of much value to me.'[18]

At an early stage Cameron's etchings were championed by P. G. Hamerton, the art critic and editor of *The Portfolio*, a monthly magazine about the arts. Hamerton illustrated 'Perth Bridge' (R.28), an early etching by Cameron, in the July 1889 issue of *The Portfolio*.[19] In his review of the 1890 annual exhibition of the RE Hamerton commented favourably on the 'Clyde Set', describing the etchings as '… picturesque illustrations of the scenery of the Clyde and elsewhere …' and he featured Cameron's Clyde etchings in the September 1892 issue, illustrating 'Arran' (R.43). Hamerton's description aptly sums up Cameron's attempts at this stage. They are little more than views, competently executed but somewhat lacking in individuality of expression. However, 'Bothwell' (R.34) and 'Greenock, No. 2' (R.58) are noteworthy. The former is a beautifully balanced composition depicting a wooded bend in the Clyde with the towers of Bothwell Castle glimpsed above the trees in the distance. The latter is a detailed architectural study of the town with sailing ships moored in the busy harbour in the foreground.

Cameron's first 'one-man' exhibition was held at the galleries of Van Baerle in Glasgow's Hope Street in December 1891. He showed some 50 etchings of Scotland and London, which he had visited for the first time in 1890, executing a number of plates depicting scenes along the River Thames, some, such as 'Thames Warehouses' (R.64), showing the influence of Whistler. The exhibition received good reviews in the local press. A reviewer in *The Bailie* described Cameron as:

'Without doubt … one of the most able and promising etchers Scotland has produced. . His manner is singularly delicate and yet strong and suggestive. He is a true artist, with no forced effects or coarseness of style. His self-restraint and grace of touch show a master hand'.[20]

The critic of the *North British Daily Mail* wrote:

'As a painter in oil Mr. Cameron has already taken a high place, and the present exhibition will greatly enhance his reputation. A glance round the walls gives a strong impression of the artist's versatility and the width of his sympathies in regard to the beautiful, the picturesque, and the humorous'.[21]

High praise indeed for a young artist. Whether the exhibition was a financial success is unknown, but it must have provided Cameron with sufficient funds to undertake an extended visit to Holland with his friend James Craig Annan the following year.

James Craig Annan (1864-1946) was the second son of the photographer Thomas Annan. When he was 19 he had gone with his father to Vienna to learn the new process of photogravure from its inventor Karl Klic, a process for which Thomas Annan had purchased the sole rights in Britain and which was to revolutionise the reproduction of works of art.[22] Annan was only a year older than Cameron and it is possible that the two met as a result of their interest in remarkably similar processes – the photogravure plate is inked and printed in the same way as an etched plate. The previous year

Annan had introduced Cameron to the work of the early photographers D. O. Hill and Robert Adamson, from whose paper negatives Annan had produced some prints in photogravure.[23] One of these – a portrait of Mrs. Anne Rigby – Cameron had reworked as an etching entitled 'Old Age' (R.84)[24]

It seems likely that their visit to Holland in the spring of 1892 was prompted by their mutual admiration for the work of the artists of the Hague School, who, as has been noted, were very popular in Scotland in the second half of the nineteenth century. The two friends toured around the north of Holland, Cameron sketching subjects as varied as a timber merchant's yard in Utrecht, buildings and canals in Amsterdam, a small courtyard in Alkmaar, the flower market in Haarlem, windmills in Zaandam and the activities of the fisher folk of Zandvoort, while Annan took his photographs, patiently waiting for long periods until the subject matter was just right. No doubt they helped and complemented each other in their work. Certainly Annan considered it important for him to be with another artist. In an address he gave at the opening of an exhibition of his work at the Royal Photographic Society in 1900 he said that when he worked with people who had 'little intimate knowledge of art, I have found the contents of my camera to be sadly lacking in that subtle something which makes one photograph so very much more interesting than another'.[25]

On his return Cameron etched the 'North Holland Set' of 22 plates, printing ten complete sets and a few individual impressions of selected items. The two friends held a joint exhibition at the newly opened gallery of T. & R. Annan & Sons in Glasgow's Sauchiehall Street. Annan exhibited about 25 of his Dutch prints, including his celebrated 'The Beach at Zandvoort' and 'On a Dutch Shore', which later were to win him international recognition. Cameron showed the 'North Holland Set', together

PLATE 10
The Windmill *1892*
Etching, 10 × 11¾
Private Collection

with a further nine etchings of Dutch subjects. These plates mark a greater maturity in terms of both technique and composition, demonstrated by, for example, 'The Windmill' (R.131, pl.10) and the wonderful 'A Rembrandt Farm' (R.139), in which Cameron pays homage to Rembrandt. That great painter and etcher was to be a source of inspiration and joy to him throughout his life. As well as lecturing on Rembrandt and other great artists, he assembled over the years a very fine collection of around 50 of Rembrandt's etchings, which he gifted to the National Gallery of Scotland in 1943.

The delicate and cleanly bitten lines of Cameron's very early plates suggest the influence of Maxime Lalanne, whose book *A Treatise on Etching* had inspired James McBey to exchange the security of a career in a bank for the life of an artist. However, it is obvious that Cameron had been studying the work of the great etchers. An important early influence was Sir Francis Seymour Haden (1818-1910), whose landscape etchings Cameron would have seen in George Stevenson's own collection. The influence of the great masters Rembrandt and Whistler has been noted already. That of the important French etcher Charles Meryon (1821-1868), famed for his plates of the buildings of Paris, may be discerned in 'Old Houses, Stirling' (R.148) of 1892-5. However, Cameron was no mere imitator. He was to develop a personal style which is instantly recognisable as pure Cameron. Something of Cameron's eventual style in landscape is seen in the rich drypoint 'Landscape with Trees' (R.151) of 1892, in which dark groups of trees on either bank of a small river are silhouetted against a clear evening sky and reflected in the still water, and 'A Border Tower' (R.196) of 1894, which is somewhat similar in composition to 'A Rembrandt Farm', with the remains of a small Border keep partly hidden by a clump of trees in a wide, flat pastoral landscape.

'The Palace, Stirling Castle' (R.174) of 1893 was, according to Rinder, the first of Cameron's etchings to attract much attention.[26] It depicts the corner of a courtyard dominated by the massive walls of James V's ornate Renaissance palace within the castle. In its printing Cameron used for the first time the technique of retroussage – passing a muslin pad lightly over the inked plate in order to drag some of the ink out of the lines and across the plate to achieve a softening of the image.

In 1894 Annan and Cameron again travelled abroad together, on this occasion going to northern Italy, visiting Genoa, Florence, Verona and Venice. Over the next two years Cameron worked on 31 plates of Italian scenes and figure studies. The latter included two portraits – 'Paolo Salviati' (R.208), a bearded monk, and 'Veronica' (R.205), a powerful portrayal of the head of a girl in profile wearing a medieval head-dress. Cameron contributed the drawing for 'Veronica' to the *Yellow Book* along with the magazine's cover design and title page in an issue given over to Glasgow artists.[27] The 'North Italian Set', comprising 26 etchings plus a portfolio label and title page, was published in 1896 by W. B. Paterson of Glasgow, the art dealer brother of Glasgow Boy James Paterson. 25 complete sets (plus several individual impressions) were printed and offered for sale at £30 per set. Such was the demand for etchings in the first three decades of the present century that one of the sets made £460 at auction in 1911 and another achieved £1,290 in 1929.[28] An exhibition of the Italian etchings was held at the London gallery of Richard Gutekunst.

Despite being well received, the set is rather mixed, both in subject matter and quality. In addition to 'Veronica' and 'Paolo Salviati', which were praised by the critics, 'The Palace Doorway' (R.225), the ornate entrance from the Grand Canal of the Palazzo Dario, 'Pastoral' (R.228) and 'Landscape with Trees' (R.229) are very fine. Several plates are let down by rather poor figures. It has to be said that Cameron was never entirely happy in his representation of the human form, either in terms of drawing or placing it within his composition. It did not come easily to him and some are more successful than others.

By this time Cameron was gaining an international reputation as an etcher. He had been awarded a Bronze Medal at the World's Columbian Exposition in Chicago in 1893. In 1895 he had his first one-man exhibition in America at the New York gallery of Frederick Keppel & Co. He showed over 90 etchings and drypoints, as well as about a dozen pencil drawings and one oil painting of a waterfront scene. The exhibition was lauded by the local press. The critic of the *Chicago Sunday Times Herald* enthused:

> 'Mr. Cameron's work is characterised by exquisite delicacy of touch. His strength is incisive and brilliant; every line is made to tell its own story. He possesses the individuality that belongs to genius. His handling of the needle not only does the duty of modelling, but of producing the effect of texture. He has imagination and the technic with which to express himself. Mr. Cameron is a master of the foundation of the graphic arts – drawing. He has a love of form and also of beauty ... .'[29]

The same year he was elected to the senior rank of a Fellow of the RE.

[1] Farington, *Diary 1793-1821*, I, quoted in David & Francina Irwin, *Scottish Painters at Home and Abroad 1700-1900*, London, 1975, p.222

[2] Roger Billcliffe, *The Royal Glasgow Institute of the Fine Arts: Dictionary of Exhibitors*, Vol. I, Glasgow, 1990, p.9

[3] Charles Dumas, 'Art Dealers and Collectors', article in *The Hague School* exhibition catalogue, Royal Academy, London, 1983, p.130

[4] Elizabeth Bird, 'International Glasgow', *Connoisseur*, August 1973, p.250

[5] J. Carfrae Alston, T. G. Arthur, A. J. Kirkpatrick, Robert Ramsey, *Fine Arts Catalogue*, International Exhibition Glasgow 1888

[6] Some may have been etchings – the catalogue is unclear

[7] Ronald Pickvance, *A Man of Influence: Alex Reid 1854-1928*, Scottish Arts Council, Edinburgh, 1967, p.6

[8] Ibid., p.7 (it seems likely that for a time Reid shared lodgings in Paris with Vincent van Gogh)

[9] Ibid., p.5

[10] *Glasgow Art Review*, Vol.I, No.1, 1946

[11] Roger Billcliffe, *The Glasgow Boys*, London, 1985, p.312

[12] St. Louis Exposition 1895, exhibition catalogue, p.7

[13] Letter from Cameron to James Connell & Sons, Glasgow, dated 12th April 1899 (NLS ACC7797.1)

[14] Letter from Cameron to Frost & Reed, Bristol, dated 13th June 1914 (NLS ACC6255)

[15] Letter from Cameron to James Connell & Sons, Glasgow, dated 24th January 1900 (NLS ACC7797.1)

[16] In 1890 a further 50 sets (unsigned) were published by E. & E. Silva White, Glasgow.

[17] Rinder (Rinder notes that 40 prints were destroyed, but does not give the reason)

[18] Letter from Cameron to James Connell & Sons, Glasgow, dated 19th February 1897

(NLS ACC7797.1)

[19] *The Portfolio* Vol.20, July 1889

[20] *The Bailie*, 16th December 1891

[21] *North British Daily Mail*, 11th December 1891

[22] William Buchanan, 'J. Craig Annan and D. Y. Cameron in North Holland', article in *British Photography in the Nineteenth Century*, edited by Mike Weaver

[23] Ibid.

[24] Hill and Adamson's 'Mrs. Rigby' is reproduced in Sara Stevenson, *David Octavius Hill and Robert Adamson*, Edinburgh, 1981

[25] Buchanan, op. cit.

[26] Rinder, p.69

[27] *Yellow Book*, vol. VIII, January 1896

[28] Harold J. L. Wright, *The Etchings & Drypoints of Sir D. Y. Cameron*, Print Collectors' Club, No. 24, London, 1947, p.13

[29] *Chicago Sunday Times Herald*, 3rd November 1895

CHAPTER FOUR

MARRIAGE AND LONDON

WHILE CAMERON WORKED VERY HARD WITH THE NEEDLE to establish a reputation as an etcher, he did not forsake the brush – far from it. The earliest known work in oil is 'Landscape' (private collection), signed 'D. Young Cameron' and dated 1883. He was then only 17 or 18 and attending classes at Glasgow School of Art in his spare time. Two lines of verse are written on a label on the back of the painting:

'The day breaks o'er the standing stones
    And bursts the night cloud dark and drear'

It appears to depict the ruins of a chambered cairn on moorland at sunrise; it may be an imaginary scene or possibly one of the many prehistoric sites on Arran, where the Cameron family spent summer holidays. 'Black-waterfoot' (1889, pl.11) shows a marked advance in both technique and composition. In subject matter and style it is quite unlike any other painting by Cameron – a charming country scene, somewhat similar to the work of the landscape artist Sam Bough (1822-1878). Cameron executed at least one further small oil of Blackwaterfoot (private collection). His etching 'Cottage, Arran: Sunset' (R.14) of 1888 depicts the same scene from a different angle. Blackwaterfoot is a hamlet on the west coast of the island. Cameron returned many times to Arran to etch and paint its scenery, particularly the rugged peaks of Cir Mhor and its neighbours in the north of the island.

In the 1890s Cameron was beginning to find his feet, producing

PLATE 11
Blackwaterfoot *1889*
Oil on canvas, 19½ × 27
Private Collection

landscapes, figure paintings and portraits in a variety of styles. In 1891 he had taken a studio at 134 Bath Street, where some ten years earlier W. Y. Macgregor had held life classes for his fellow Glasgow Boys. The work of the Boys, particularly in their later decorative phase, and of the artists of the Hague School were important influences on Cameron during this period. Something of James Guthrie and E. A. Walton can be seen in 'Anemones' (c.1893, pl.12), which Cameron exhibited at the Walker Art Gallery in Liverpool in 1893. 'The White Butterfly' (c.1894, whereabouts unknown) and 'Fairy Lilian' (c.1895, pl.13) are in the style of the Hague School painter Matthijs Maris (1839-1917), the brother of the artists Jacob and Willem Maris. 'Fairy Lilian', which has echos of Maris's mystical 'The Church Bride' in the Mesdag Collection in The Hague, was exhibited at the RGI in 1895 and the RSA in 1896. It received favourable reviews in the press, despite being poorly hung at the RSA. Commenting on Cameron's work at the RGI, the critic of the *North British Daily Mail* waxed lyrical:

> 'Let the visitor pass to the 'Fairy Lilian' of D. Y. Cameron, an artist who first made his name as an etcher and who is now doing excellent work in colour. His 'Fairy Lilian' recalls the poet's vision of the maiden with 'crimson-threaded lips' here jewelled and robed in scarlet and gold, with lace falling from the shoulder in folds light as gossamer. It is a dream-like presentation of an ideal maiden swathed in soft mystery. The colour is extremely refined, and beautiful in its very indefiniteness.'[1]

The painting was purchased by the Glasgow collector James Carfrae Alston,

PLATE 12 (LEFT)
Anemones c.1893
Oil on canvas, 36 × 36
Bourne Fine Art

PLATE 13
Fairy Lilian c.1895
Oil on canvas, 34½ × 23½
Glasgow Art Gallery & Museum

who gifted it to Kelvingrove Art Gallery in 1909. 'The White Butterfly' is very similar to Maris's 'The Butterflies' (1874, Burrell, Glasgow), which was owned by the Glasgow collector Thomas Glenn Arthur and later by Sir William Burrell. Cameron would have seen the painting when it was exhibited at the Glasgow International Exhibition in 1888. After being ignored for a period, the work of Matthijs Maris had come to the fore again in the early 1890s and his dream landscapes and mystical maidens influenced a number of artists. It is just possible that Cameron's sister Katharine may have reintroduced her brother to the work of Maris. As will be appreciated later, Maris and the Dutch symbolist painter Jan Toorop were among a number of artists who had an influence on the ideas of a small circle of students at Glasgow School of Art in the mid-1890s, one of whom was Katharine. The influence of the more traditional artists of the Hague School, such as Jacob Maris (1837-1899), Hendrik Willem Mesdag (1831-1915) and J. H. Weissenbruch (1824-1903), is to be seen in Cameron's fine waterfront scenes such as 'A French Harbour' (1894, Hunterian, Glasgow), 'The Old Harbour' (1894, untraced) and 'South Coast Harbour' (c.1896, pl.14).[2]

Cameron executed a number of portraits and figure studies during the 1890s. Some are successful, others less so. 'Mrs. Thomas Annan' (1894, Kelvingrove, Glasgow), the mother of James Craig Annan portrayed in Dutch dress, is very much in the manner of Whistler's 'Arrangement in Grey and Black: Portrait of the Painter's Mother' of 1871. Cameron's portrait appears rather stiff; it was not liked by the Annan family. However,

PLATE 14
South Coast Harbour c.1896
Oil on canvas, 24½ × 37½
Private Collection

when it was exhibited at the Salon, Champ de Mars in Paris in 1897, it attracted favourable comment from the correspondent of *The Scotsman*:

> '… It is an artistic piece of work. The figure is well drawn, the face nicely and softly modelled, and a reposeful air pervades the canvas, which has excellent tone'.[3]

On the other hand, Cameron's 'Dorothy Maude Kay' (1898, pl.16) is excellent. It is a charming portrait of a young girl of nine or ten, the only child of the Glasgow merchant and art connoisseur Arthur Kay and his first wife, executed in the style of Velasquez, interest in whom had been stimulated by the publication three years earlier of R. A. M. Stevenson's biography. It is very similar to work being done around the same time by Dundee-born artist William James Yule.[4] It was exhibited in 1898 at the New Gallery in London, along with another portrait 'Morag' (untraced). The correspondent of the *New York Tribune* commented favourably on both paintings:

> 'There are two pictures by Mr. Cameron which are of great promise. One is a portrait of Dorothy Maude Kay … there is an exquisite sense of color …. The second picture, entitled 'Morag', presents a girl with dark hair and dreamy eyes, with a harmonious combination of pale shades of pink and dull red finely blended. This young Scotch artist has been chiefly known to us as an etcher but he has suddenly produced two works in a distinctive style of his own, which is not an imitation of Velasquez. The technique is excellent and the treatment highly poetic'.[5]

In 1896 Cameron married Jeanie Ure Maclaurin, the eldest of the three daughters of Robert Maclaurin and his wife Margaret Anderson. Their

PLATE 15 (ABOVE)
Lady Cameron c.1900
T. & R. Annan & Sons Ltd

PLATE 16 (LEFT)
Dorothy Maude Kay *1898*
Oil on canvas, 34 × 40
Private Collection

PLATE 17
Dieppe Castle *1896*
Pencil and wash, 11 × 15
Flemings

wedding day – April 30th – was the same day on which Jeanie's parents had been married 29 years earlier. Cameron had met Jeanie in 1889, when he was 24 and she was 18.[6] A year or so earlier the Maclaurins had moved from Balloch at the south end of Loch Lomond, where Jeanie was born, to Great George Street in Glasgow's Hillhead. Their house was just round the corner from 10 South Park Terrace, to which the Camerons moved shortly thereafter. They were a well-to-do middle class family. Jeanie's paternal grandfather, like Cameron's father, had been a United Presbyterian minister. Her father was a partner in Archibald Orr Ewing and Company in the Vale of Leven, one of the largest Turkey Red dyers and printers in the world, employing in those days a workforce of several thousands.

The couple spent their honeymoon in Rouen in northern France, travelling via Dieppe.[7] Cameron's watercolour 'Dieppe Castle' (pl.17) dates from this visit – he did an etching of the scene (R.274) the following year. Although no oils or watercolours are known to have been executed in Rouen, he must have produced a number of sketches, which formed the basis for several etchings over the next two years, including 'Old Houses, Rouen' (R.275), which shows the influence of Meryon, and 'The Crucifix' (R.281), depicting the interior of the church of St. Maclou in Rouen, the crucifix with winged angels either side, above a slender decorated arch, silhouetted against the light from the high east window.

The Camerons set up house at 12 St. James's Terrace (now called Ruskin Terrace) on the north side of Great Western Road, only a short distance from the homes of both families. Cameron had a large studio built in the garden to the rear, the interior being designed by Charles Rennie Mackintosh, who was known to Cameron's sister Katharine and probably to Cameron himself.[8] However, they did not stay there long, for in 1898 they decided to move from Glasgow to London, taking rooms in Markham Square in Chelsea. By that time the majority of the Boys had left Glasgow; several, such as Lavery, Melville and Walton, had made for London where financial success, if not critical acclaim, was more assured. The house in St. James's Terrace was sold to Dr. Alexander Frew, who married the artist Bessie MacNicol in 1899.

The same year (1898) Cameron showed three paintings – 'Daisy' (1897, untraced), 'Braxfield' (1898, Dublin) and 'Portrait of a Lady' (1898, untraced) – at the inaugural exhibition of the International Society of Sculptors, Painters and Gravers in Knightsbridge. The International, as it came to be known, had been founded that year by Whistler, who was elected as its President with John Lavery as Vice-President. It was an anti-Academy society, rather like the New English Art Club, which had been established in 1886. Other founder members included Joseph Crawhall, David Gauld, James Guthrie, Arthur Melville and E. A. Walton. Over the next few years most of the other Glasgow Boys, with the exception of W. Y. Macgregor, were elected to membership. Cameron became a member in 1901 and served on its Council for a period. He was to exhibit work on an irregular basis until 1919.

It was intended that the artists invited to exhibit at the International should represent the best of non-Academy art and be drawn from many countries. However, it never fulfilled the promise of its first exhibition. It was perceived initially as an exhibiting society for Whistler and his followers. After his death in 1903 the International eventually settled for a position somewhere between the RA and the New English Art Club. Ironically, its 29th and final exhibition in 1925 was held at the RA, the very body the International had sought to rival.

In April 1899 Cameron had a one-man exhibition at the galleries of P. & D. Colnaghi in London's Pall Mall. It was a most important event for him – the first occasion on which collectors and critics had been able to judge more than two or three of his paintings at one time. He had worked very hard to put together a substantial body of work and their reaction would have been eagerly awaited. He showed fourteen oils – all completed within the last two years, of which seven had not been exhibited before – as well as etchings and a large number of drawings in pencil and black chalk, mainly sketches of Italian subjects executed on his visit to northern Italy in 1894 for translation into etchings.

There were four portraits, three figure studies, including 'The Bride' (1897, Adelaide), four landscapes with figures, including two major works – 'The Avenue' (1898, whereabouts unknown) and 'The Bridge' (c.1898, Munich) – and three landscapes.[9] Overall, it was an impressive showing. Cameron was a Romantic – a colourist with a broad, decorative style. There were many excellent reviews. But some of the more discerning critics noted a certain lack of substance – truth sacrificed to decoration and an artificial elegance. The critic of *The Art Journal* wrote:

> 'The collection at Messrs Colnaghi's fully justified Mr. Cameron's reputation as
> a painter of breadth and style. He is more grand than accurate in conception,
> and the magnificent manner of his canvases fits them for the society of pictures
> by such great men as Rousseau, Corot, Courbet, and Millet. But one might find
> him shallow in such company; he lacks those men's knowledge of nature, he

treats the features of landscape and man somewhat largely and summarily as elements of a decorative scheme. The dignity of his work commands instant respect, gives tone to surroundings, and acts upon you with something of the effect of noble oratory or great rhetoric. Conventionality, however, is more apparent in it than in the true intimate poetry of nature given us by such a man as Corot'.[10]

The critic of the *Manchester Guardian* wrote in a similar vein:

'The small exhibition of pictures by Mr. D. Y. Cameron at Messrs. Colnaghi's Galleries in Pall Mall suggests rather than displays capacity in the artist. Mr. Cameron is a better colourist than painter; he is a still better draughtsman and etcher. In his pictures the cool schemes and the studied, Velasquez-like tones which he affects are always grateful to the eye. But when one looks into the painting itself one too often finds that the structure is flimsy, the brush-drawing only at times respectable, the command of texture never first-rate ... Mr. Cameron relies too easily on the accomplishment that he undoubtedly possesses, and does not seem to be vigorously in search of firmer ground on which to build up his future'.[11]

Writing in the *Pall Mall Gazette*, the critic R. A. M. Stevenson called into question Cameron's abilities as a portrait painter:

'He lacks the special virtues of the portrait maker – subtlety of modelling, preference of structure before style, love of intimate character rather than grand manner'.[12]

However, the two major works in the exhibition – 'The Bridge' and 'The Avenue' – appear to have received more acclaim on the Continent. The former was exhibited at the Munich Secession in 1899, when the correspondent of *The Studio* reported that it was 'the delight and admiration of all beholders'; the painting was purchased by the city's art gallery.[13] When 'The Avenue' was exhibited in Paris in 1900, the critic of the *New York Times* enthused about it:

'Cameron's 'Avenue', a deep umbrageous avenue in a park, with distinguished men and women sitting about it in 1830s costumes, is, however, a revelation and a marvel, a pure chef d'oeuvre by a great painter, intelligent and sensitive beyond praise, with something of Fragonard and a good deal of Charles Conder in his undoubted genius'.[14]

Cameron also exhibited 'The Avenue' at the World's Fair in St. Louis in 1904.

Whether the exhibition at Colnaghi was a financial success is not known; unfortunately, the gallery's records have been lost. What Cameron's feelings were can only be guessed. However, it is significant that with one exception – showing 'Dorothy Maude Kay' at the RGI in 1900 – he never exhibited another portrait or figure study. From then on he concentrated on what he liked doing best – landscapes and architectural subjects.

However, if the critics were mixed in their reactions to his oil paintings, their opinions of his etchings were much more positive. His reputation as an

1 *North British Daily Mail*, ? February 1896
2 The location of the harbour is unknown; it looks more like a Scottish harbour than one on the south coast
3 *The Scotsman*, 24th April 1897
4 See *William James Yule*, Pyms Gallery, London, 1983
5 *New York Tribune*, ?1 May 1898
6 An etching entitled 'Jean' (R.61) was executed in 1890 and exhibited at the RE in 1891
7 Rev. Robert James Gordon Watt, Cameron's great-nephew, believes that Katharine accompanied the couple on their honeymoon to Rouen, which could account for the subsequent coolness between the two women
8 Ailsa Tanner, *West of Scotland Women Artists*, Helensburgh & District Art Club, 1976, p.20
9 Full list of oil paintings exhibited at Colnaghi: 'The Avenue' (c.1898), 'Boquhapple' (c.1898), 'Braxfield' (1898), 'The Bride' (1897), 'The Bridge' (c.1898), 'The Dreamer' (c.1898), 'A French River' (1898), 'Gipsy' (1898), 'Master Willie' (c.1898), 'Menteith' (c.1898), 'Portrait of a Lady' (1898), 'Robert Meldrum, Esq' (1898), 'Rosamund' (c.1898), 'The Woodland Mirror' (c.1898)
10 *The Art Journal*, June 1899
11 *Manchester Guardian*, 17th April 1899
12 *Pall Mall Gazette*, 18th April 1899
13 *The Studio*, Vol. 17, 1899 (illustrated)
14 *New York Times*, 11th July 1900
15 Dundee: Mr. Robert Scott, 19 Albert Square; Aberdeen: Hay & Lyall's Royal Fine Art Gallery
16 Arthur M. Hind, *Etchings of D. Y. Cameron*, London, 1924, p.22

etcher was blossoming. Following his Bronze Medal in Chicago in 1893, he was awarded a Silver Medal at Exposition Internationale Beaux Arts at Brussels and a Gilt Medal at Erste Internationale Kunstausstellung in Dresden in 1897 – in both instances Cameron was the only British etcher to receive a medal. That year he had a joint exhibition with his sister Katharine at Richard Gutekunst's gallery in King Street. Over the next year or so his etchings were shown at Dotts' Gallery in Edinburgh and at the Renfield Street gallery of James Connell & Sons in Glasgow, as well as at galleries in Dundee and Aberdeen.[15] The exhibitions were well received by the local press and further confirmed Cameron's position as one of the most promising of the younger etchers.

Throughout the second half of the 1890s Cameron continued with his etching. In addition to the etchings of Dieppe and Rouen already mentioned, his work included the wonderful landscape 'Ledaig' (R.278) and the architectural studies 'A Venetian Palace' (R.282), 'The Palace of the Stuarts' (R.285) and 'Broad Street, Stirling' (R.286). The latter highlight his love for architecture. His skill in depicting the precise character of a building was to be seen fully for the first time in some of his etchings of London subjects executed in 1899. The 'London Set' of 12 etchings was published by Richard Gutekunst in 1900. 35 complete sets, together with a few individual impressions of each subject, were printed and signed by Cameron. 'St. Paul's from the Thames' (R.299) is a fine etching touched with drypoint in the style of Whistler. However, it is 'The Admiralty' (R.293), 'Waterloo Bridge, No.2' (R.296) and 'Newgate' (R.300) which show Cameron at his most impressive to date, all powerful examples of his feeling for the subject and demonstrating 'the true kinship with Meryon and the great masters who have brought dead stones to life'.[16]

PLATE 18
Holyrood Palace *1896*
Ink and wash, 10½ × 18
Flemings

CHAPTER FIVE

KIPPEN

AROUND THE MIDDLE OF 1899 THE CAMERONS RETURNED to Scotland. Why they decided to leave London is unknown. Perhaps they had intended to stay only a short time or it may not have worked out in the way they had hoped. However, it seems most likely that one or both of them got homesick for Scotland and their families and friends.

The couple moved to Kippen, a small village near Stirling, where they were to live for the rest of their lives. The village stands on a north-facing slope with wonderful views stretching from Ben Lomond in the west to Stirling Castle on its crag in the east. For the first three years they lived at Kirkhill, a large house on the eastern edge of the village.

Cameron's pattern of work continued along much the same lines as previously in Glasgow. He pushed forward with both his painting and his etching, exhibiting his work at the RSA and the RGI in Scotland, in London at the RE, the International and the Society of Oil Painters, and in Liverpool at the annual Autumn Exhibition held at the Walker Art Gallery. Occasionally, he exhibited overseas. His work was increasingly selected for favourable comment by the critics in their exhibition reviews in art periodicals such as *The Studio* and *The Art Journal.*

During the first decade of the present century, the Camerons continued to go abroad regularly. In March 1900 they travelled to Italy, visiting Siena,

PLATE 19
Kirkhill *1899*
Oil on canvas, 17 x 19
Clydesdale Bank

Florence and Venice. On their return Cameron etched eight plates of architectural subjects, including 'Siena' (R.304, pl.20) with its varying light and shadow, 'The Rialto' (R.305), seen from a very unusual angle, and 'Saint Mark's No. 2' (R.307, pl.21), the glowing light from its magnificent rose window illuminating the interior of the basilica and the figures of the worshippers, insignificant in comparison with the massive proportions of the building. Architecture is well suited to the medium of etching and Cameron conveys not only the beauty of a building, but also something of its history and its mystery – almost its soul. 'Saint Mark's No.2' is an early example of one of Cameron's church interiors, a subject which became a favourite with him. Over a period extending from 1895 to 1931 he executed a number of interiors in etching and drypoint, watercolour and oil, including his celebrated etching 'The Five Sisters, York Minster' (R.397) of 1907, the watercolour 'Notre Dame de la Couture' (1909, pl.22) and his Diploma oils of the cathedrals of Winchester and Durham, which, under the rules of both Academies, Cameron was obliged to lodge with the RSA and the RA when he was elected an Academician in 1918 and 1920 respectively.

In his church interiors he liked to contrast the irregular pattern of light cast from a window, seen or unseen, with the dark richness of the shadows. Often he accentuated the mass and strength of the structure, its arches and soaring columns. The beauty of the stonework in a simple arch in a church or in the complex geometry of a corner or a crossing in a lofty cathedral is lovingly depicted in light golden brown or in mellowed ivory.

The influence of David Roberts (1796-1864) can be seen in some of Cameron's work. He would have been familiar with the architectural studies and church interiors of Roberts from the numerous engravings of his work, as well as with the lithographs of his landscapes, which appeared in books such as *Landscape Illustrations of the Bible* published in 1836 and which may very well have had a place in the library of a scholarly man like the Rev. Robert Cameron. Cameron's father also may have had a portfolio of Louis Haghe's lithographs of the drawings of the Holy Land by Roberts. It is easy to imagine Cameron as a boy avidly scanning the plates in the books in his father's study.

However, it was Johannes Bosboom (1817-1891), the Hague School artist who specialised in church interiors, who was the principal influence on Cameron. He would have seen Bosboom's work at the International Exhibitions in Edinburgh and Glasgow in 1886 and 1888 respectively, as well as on his visit to Holland with James Craig Annan in 1892. Work by Bosboom also was to be seen occasionally at the annual exhibitions of the RGI.

Nevertheless, Cameron's interiors are very much his own and not mere imitations of those of Roberts or Bosboom. They range from the stark simplicity of a small rural church to the awesome richness and colour of a great continental cathedral. The latter is exemplified in 'St. Mark's, Evening' (1901, untraced), which he exhibited at the Society of Oil Painters in 1901 and which was praised by the press, the critic of *The Art Journal* commenting:

'The work of another Scotsman is arresting .... The relationships between colour and colour, between deep shadow and late sunlight filtered through the windows of St. Mark's, have been sensitively felt and are well conveyed'.[1]

Cameron's interest in church interiors was not restricted to depicting them on paper or on canvas. He believed that beauty and decoration were essential elements in the symbolism of worship, which he considered very important. He regretted the extremes of the Reformation, which resulted in the destruction of so much church ornamentation and symbolism. In later life he advocated embellishment of Scottish churches, acting as vice-convenor of the Church of Scotland's Advisory Committee on Artistic Questions from 1934 to his death in 1945 and advising many churches on their plans for refurbishment. Kippen Parish Church was renovated in the 1920s, relying heavily on his advice and resources.

Early in May 1902 the Camerons were in Paris, prior to setting out for Chartres and a journey through the ancient provinces of Touraine and Anjou in north-west France. The places which they visited in the valley of the Loire are known from the series of etchings which Cameron produced on his return – Blois, Amboise, Tours, Loches, Chinon, Saumur and Angers. In his etchings he is much more interested in depicting the rich architecture of the medieval buildings lining the narrow streets than the massive chateau or citadel which dominates almost every one of those towns. Cameron is a master of detail and mood. 'Angers:Rue des Filles Dieu' (R.329) depicts a typical medieval street, lined by a motley collection of old buildings, some of which cast a dark shadow over a portion of the narrow roadway and the wall of the houses opposite. 'Place Plumereau, Tours' (R.353) shows a cluster of old buildings in a variety of styles. 'St. Laumer,Blois' (R.351) is a fine church interior, looking from the nave, bathed in light, towards the rich dark shadows of the lofty choir, with the crucifix in the background silhouetted against a source of light.

Cameron is more expansive in his watercolours and oils. 'Amboise' (1902, pl.23) is a beautiful watercolour of the late Gothic and Renaissance chateau seen from across the Loire; it was a favourite royal residence – the French Kings Charles VIII and Francis I brought artists and artisans from

PLATE 20 (ABOVE OPPOSITE)
Siena *1900*
Etching touched with drypoint, 11¼ × 5⅝
Private Collection

PLATE 21 (BELOW OPPOSITE)
Saint Mark's No.2 *1900*
Etching, 12 × 7¾
Private Collection

PLATE 22 (ABOVE)
Notre Dame de la Couture *c.1909*
Watercolour over pencil, 28 × 16½
Manchester City Art Galleries

PLATE 23 (LEFT)
Amboise *1903*
Watercolour, 4 × 9
Private Collection

Italy to embellish the castle in the late 15th and early 16th centuries. He exhibited an oil 'The Square, Amboise' in Budapest in 1903, which was purchased for the city's Museum of Fine Arts. His sunlit canvas 'St. Hubert's, Amboise' was bought for the civic art gallery in Durban, South Africa the same year. The oil 'A Britanny Farm' (pl.25) probably dates from this period, although it is possible that it could be earlier – Cameron rarely dated his work and in many instances it is impossible to be anything other than approximate in determining the year of execution. The small oil 'A Courtyard in Blois' (*c.*1903, pl.24) is a charming scene on a domestic scale. On the other hand the low-toned oil 'Dark Angers' (1903, pl.26) is a

powerful architectural study on a grand scale. The former capital of Anjou is dominated by the mellow stonework of the bridge across the River Maine and the dark round towers and other buildings of the massive castle rising up behind it. Cameron exhibited the painting at the annual exhibition of the Society of Oil Painters in 1903, when the critic of *The Art Journal* described it as 'among the most impressive exhibits' and then added 'impressive, that is, rather than enchanting'.[2] 'Spring Blossoms, Touraine' (1903, untraced), depicting a wide, sunlit road, flanked on the left by tall trees which cast slender shadows across it, winding towards a village dominated by a large chateau, also was exhibited at the Society in 1903. In subject matter – the awakening of the landscape in springtime after the slumber of winter – and in composition it is very similar to 'Early Spring in Tuscany' (c. 1901, untraced). Cameron had executed the latter following their travels through northern Italy in 1900. He exhibited the painting at the Society in 1902, prompting the critic of *The Art Journal* to write 'Were there no other picture here, the gallery should be visited to see this work of Mr. Cameron'.[3]

Cameron had exhibited at the Society of Oil Painters for the first time in 1901. The Society had been very much a second rank institution, being neither the prime 'establishment' exhibiting society nor a progressive society like the International or the New English Art Club. Indeed, *The Art Journal* described its exhibitions as 'almost uniformly commonplace'.[4] In an attempt to rectify this, the Society's Council had encouraged many of the younger Scottish artists to submit work and in 1902 had elected several of them to membership, including Thomas Austen Brown (who resigned almost immediately), John Lavery and Cameron. It would appear that Cameron had second thoughts and ceased to exhibit with the Society after 1904, although he served on its Council from 1904 to 1906.

In 1903 Cameron and fellow Scot William Strang (1859-1921) resigned as Fellows of the RE in protest at the Council's decision to admit to the Society's exhibitions reproductions – etchings and engravings of other artists' work – and to elect such etchers and engravers as members. They

PLATE 27 (ABOVE)
Rue St Julien-le-Pauvre, Paris *1903*
Watercolour, 9 × 6¾
Glasgow Art Gallery & Museum

PLATE 28 (LEFT)
A Norman Village *1903*
Watercolour, 12 × 16
Untraced

PLATE 29 (RIGHT)
Doge's Palace *1902*
Etching touched with drypoint, 10 × 15¾
Garton & Co

were concerned also with the autocratic manner of the President, Sir Francis Seymour Haden, who by then was 82. Both men felt very strongly that all prints exhibited should be original and not mere copies of someone else's work. These arguments had been rumbling on for years, when in 1902 the Council decided to go ahead with the extension of the Society's scope and objects. The loss of Cameron and Strang was very serious for the RE, as was acknowledged in its *History* published in 1930.[5] Strang was a founder member; Cameron had been elected in 1889. Both men had been ardent supporters and seldom had failed to send in work to its exhibitions.

In May of the same year the Camerons returned to France, staying mainly in Paris, but also visiting a number of places in eastern Normandy. They also went to Cluny, a small town some way south of Paris, to see the ruins of the great Benedictine abbey founded in 910, which played such a key role in reforming monasticism in the early Middle Ages. On their return to Kippen Cameron etched plates of tranquil cloisters in Montivilliers (R.355) – also the subject of a watercolour in Kelvingrove Art Gallery, Glasgow and an oil painting in the Hunterian Art Gallery, Glasgow – and a very ornate Gothic doorway in Harfleur (R.356), two towns close to Le Havre. Having resigned from the RE, Cameron decided to exhibit both etchings at the RA in London in 1904. He had had a watercolour of Venice hung at the Academy the previous year, but did not show further work until 1911, when he became a regular exhibitor, missing only three annual exhibitions in the period up to 1939.

The publication in 1903 of a catalogue of Cameron's etchings by (Sir) Frederick Wedmore, the writer and art critic, further confirmed his position as an etcher of importance in the minds of both collectors and the public at large. In an introductory note Wedmore commented that Cameron had come a long way from the tentative plates of the 'Clyde Set':

> 'And, gradually, a youth of many deficiencies and some parts, became a man of great parts and some deficiencies; and the man of great parts and of some deficiencies has become in his mature labours a veritable Master'.[6]

In the second half of that year the Camerons moved into 'Dun Eaglais', the Gaelic for 'church hill'. Designed by the architect Charles E. Whitelaw, the house had been built for them on sloping ground immediately to the north-east of Kirkhill on land purchased from the owners of Kirkhill. A carved stone plaque on the outside wall above the entrance to the house records the year 1903 and their entwined initials. Several other carved plaques bearing short texts from the Bible were incorporated in the outside walls at various times. Dun Eaglais was to be their home for the remainder of their lives. It is in a wonderful position. The principal rooms look north across the broad valley of the River Forth to the mountains of the Trossachs and the dark mass of Ben Ledi – 'The Hill of God' – traditionally the site of ancient Beltane ceremonies. It is a magnificent backdrop and in all its moods it never failed to inspire Cameron. To the east there is an equally fine view along the flanks of the Gargunnock Hills to Stirling Castle in the distance.

Extensively remodelled and extended in 1911, 1913 and 1923-4 to designs by Alexander Paterson, the architect brother of Glasgow Boy James Paterson, and by Cameron himself, Dun Eaglais is an interesting house, rather than a lovely one. At the north-east end of the house a large studio was added, probably in the 1920s. It has a very large window facing north, framing Ben Ledi in the distance. Sir James Caw recollected that the studio was 'kept spotlessly clean and tidy and with no pictures standing in it, as I remember it. But he was not greatly given to taking visitors to the studio…'.[7] Beneath the studio is a cellar, where Cameron kept his printing press.

The house was filled with fine things – furniture from the Edinburgh firm of Whytock & Reid, numerous Persian carpets and rugs and a wide assortment of books, drawings and prints, bronzes, metalwork and other objets d'art, which demonstrated a high degree of discernment and taste. However, this made it an uncomfortable house for young visitors, as Cameron's nephew Robert Cameron Watt recalled. When he visited Dun Eaglais as a child in the early years of the century, his widowed mother – Cameron's sister Marie – was terrified that he would knock into something and damage it.[8] Several rooms were 'out of bounds' to children.

PLATE 30
Linlithgow c.1904
Watercolour over charcoal, 5½ x 8¾
Flemings

The house seems much too large for a couple – the Camerons never had any children. However, they often had members of their families or friends staying with them. Sir James Guthrie, who was President of the RSA from 1902 to 1919, and Frank Rinder and his wife were frequent visitors. The Camerons had a surprisingly large domestic staff – at one time they employed two gardeners and a chauffeur, who lived either in the lodge or in the village, and a cook, a housemaid and one or two other maids, who lived in the house.

Life at Dun Eaglais was recalled in an article in *The British Weekly* by Florence Robertson Cameron, the widow of Cameron's brother James:

'Dun Eaglais was the acme of hospitality. But everything was conducted with proper laws and ceremonies – no slipshod hours, nor vague arrangements! Guests were expected to appear for prayers at a quarter to eight and for breakfast at the hour! First the family, the guests and the servants were summoned to the library, and then the 'master' read a chosen portion of Scripture, and offered a prayer for the day. Many of the prayers were specially chosen, and edited!'[9]

To people who did not know him, Cameron must have seemed stern and unbending. However, to his friends he was an interesting and charming man. In a letter to *The Times* following his death a friend wrote:

'... D. Y. was the gayest, and in every sense the best, of company, for there seemed to be a magnet in him which had power to draw out whatever of good might be lurking in others'.[10]

Cameron was a good conversationalist, but he was intolerant of trivia. He had a comic side to his nature, which revealed itself occasionally in his portrayal of a drunk precentor, though his wife disapproved.[11]

A lovely garden was carved out of the hillside, extending to about three and a half acres with roses and many specimen trees and shrubs. Andrew Kerr, the head gardener, joined straight from Stirling High School in 1903 aged 14 and was employed by the Camerons and successive owners for 56 years until his retiral in 1960. His son James Kerr recalls that Dun Eaglais

PLATE 31
The Citadel *1905*
Watercolour
Untraced

won many prizes at the annual flower shows held at Kippen and Stirling. Flowers from the garden were carried down to the church on Saturday mornings, often being arranged by Cameron himself.

To buy land and have a house designed and built, let alone filled with fine things, costs a great deal of money. Jean Cameron's parents were well off and no doubt in the early days of the marriage, particularly when the Camerons lived in their first home in St. James's Terrace in Glasgow and Cameron was struggling to make his way as an artist, they must have been very supportive. However, after the turn of the century things got better for Cameron. He found that he could sell all the prints he was able to produce. His watercolours and oils also were selling well, judging from letters which he wrote to James Connell:

> 'My large picture of 'Dark Angers' has been bought by the Corporation of Manchester to hang in their splendid collection. All my things seem to be going so easily at last.'[12]

PLATE 32
In Ely Cathedral *1904*
Oil on canvas, 23½ x 17½
Private Collection

As his reputation grew, he was able to charge more for his work. At the end of 1905 Connell was to sell 'A Castle of the Ardennes' for two hundred guineas, a not inconsiderable sum in those days.[13] He could also afford to refuse offers he considered too low:

> 'I had a wire last night from the International with an offer of £110 for my 'Glencaple' but I wired a refusal at once … I am determined to stand out against these offers. £150 is low enough but people's desires for reductions are wonderful. This is the 3rd or 4th offer of £110 which I have had for the picture.'[14]

Over a period Cameron's etchings and paintings made him a comparatively wealthy man. He was well able to sustain a sizeable establishment at Dun Eaglais, a house in London in the 1920s, and be chauffeured around Britain and the Continent in his Daimler.

1904 saw the completion of the 'Paris Set' of six etchings, published by A. Strolin in Paris in an edition of 35 sets. The Set includes two noteworthy etchings touched with drypoint – 'Saint Germain l'Auxerrois' (R.362, pl.33) depicting the slender bell-tower of the church from which the signal for the Massacre of St. Bartholomew's Day was given in 1572, and 'Hotel de Sens' (R.363). The oil 'Chateau Gaillard' (Kirkcaldy), depicting the ruins of the massive fortress built in 1196 by Richard the Lionheart on the chalk cliffs above the village of Le Petit-Andely on the Seine, and the water-colours 'Rue Saint Julien le Pauvre, Paris' (pl.27) and 'A Norman Village' (pl.28), Le Grand-Andely between Rouen and Paris, date from 1903 or 1904. Both the watercolours were used as studies for two etchings with identical titles executed in 1904 (R.366 and R.359).

From letters which Cameron wrote to James Connell, it is known that the Camerons visited York, Lincoln and Ely in May 1904. The oil 'In Ely Cathedral' (pl.32) dates from this visit. The same year, as a direct result of their resignation from the RE the previous year, Cameron and Strang joined forces with ten other artists in the formation of a new body, called The Society of Twelve, to promote the original print, whether it be etching, engraving, lithograph or woodcut. From the outset an important feature of this exhibiting society was that members could show drawings as well as prints. The founder members included some of the foremost British artists of the period. They were (in the order in which they appear in the catalogue of the Society's first exhibition):

George Clausen	Gordon Craig
William Nicholson	William Strang
Thomas Sturge Moore	William Rothenstein
Charles Ricketts	D. Y. Cameron
Charles Shannon	Augustus John
Charles Conder	Muirhead Bone

The first exhibition was held at the galleries of Obach & Co. in London's New Bond Street in 1904. A further seven exhibitions were held. Clausen, Moore, Cameron and Bone exhibited work on each occasion. As some of the founder members dropped out, they were replaced by the likes of Francis Dodd, whose etched portrait of Cameron is the frontispiece of this

PLATE 33
Saint Germain l'Auxerrois *1904*
Etching touched with drypoint, 12½ x 6⅜
Garton & Co

biography, Harvard Thomas, William Orpen and Walter Richard Sickert, the number of artists showing at each exhibition varying from nine to fourteen at the final exhibition in 1915. The Society's exhibitions did much to stimulate interest in contemporary prints and drawings.

Cameron completed two major oil paintings of Scottish subjects in 1905 – 'Glencaple' (pl.35), looking from the village of Glencaple across the estuary of the Nith to the hills of Kirkcudbrightshire, and 'St. Andrews' (Walker, Liverpool), an atmospheric view of the harbour at dusk with the square late-11th century St. Rule's Tower and the ruins of the cathedral in the background. Sunrise and sunset were mystical times of the day for Cameron; he delighted in depicting in both his paintings and his etchings the varying effects of light at those times. For several years Cameron had been much more concerned with tone than with colour. Almost all his oil paintings of the period are low in tone. Some, such as 'St. Andrews', appear over-dark; brown in various tones was the predominant colour. Indeed, he was asked occasionally to lighten a painting:

> 'On my return to Kippen [from Chartres] at the end of May I shall be very pleased to revise the picture and do what seems to me to be necessary to brighten it'.[15]

Although his tone started to lighten somewhat around 1908, it was not until the 1920s that, under the influence of the intense light of Provence and Italy, he adopted a much brighter palette.

In May 1905 the Camerons were on the Continent again, travelling throughout Belgium. The places they visited were in almost every corner of that country and included Bruges and Damme, now a small village but once the bustling port for Bruges, Brussels, Dinant on the River Meuse with its eleventh century citadel atop steep limestone cliffs some 300 feet above the town, La Roche-en-Ardenne on the River Ourthe not far from the border with Luxembourg, and Ypres. Over the following two years their travels in

PLATE 34 (OPPOSITE)
Church Interior c.1904
Watercolour, 17¾ × 12
Kirkcaldy Museum and Art Gallery

PLATE 35 (LEFT)
Glencaple 1905
Oil on canvas, 30 × 40¼
National Gallery of Scotland

PLATE 36 (OPPOSITE)
Old Brussels c.1906
Oil on canvas, 29¼ × 24¼
Private Collection

PLATE 37 (LEFT)
Laroche 1905
Watercolour, 11½ × 14½
Private Collection

PLATE 38 (BELOW)
The Meuse 1907
Etching and drypoint, 6½ × 14⅞
Garton & Co

Belgium produced a rich crop of oils, watercolours and etchings. The oils 'Old Brussels' (pl.36) and 'A Castle of the Ardennes' (1905, untraced) were exhibited at the RSA in 1906. The watercolours 'The Citadel' (pl.31) and 'Laroche' (pl.37) were exhibited at the RSW in 1905 and 1906 respectively. The 'Belgian Set' of ten etchings was published by James Connell & Sons of Glasgow and London in 1907 and formed the centrepiece of an exhibition of Cameron's etchings at Connells' London galleries the same year. 53 complete sets were printed, as well as a number of individual impressions of some of the plates. The Set is of a consistently high quality. The etching and drypoint 'The Meuse' (R.390, pl.38) is one of Cameron's best early landscapes with its simplicity and nobility of design, its rich tones and its veil of romance. Other noteworthy plates are 'Damme' (R.391) and 'Notre Dame, Dinant' (R.394), an etching touched with drypoint which must rank with 'Saint Mark's No.2', 'St. Laumer, Blois' and 'The Five Sisters, York Minster' as Cameron's finest church interiors. The Belgian Set was the final 'set' of etchings to be produced by Cameron. Over

the previous few years the emphasis had been switched from etching to painting. From 1908 to 1917, when pressure of other work forced him to forsake the needle for a period, he was to execute an average of only six plates a year.

Cameron painted at Coldstream and Berwick-upon-Tweed in 1905 and in Yorkshire the following year. His oils 'Berwick Bridge' (Flemings) and 'Early Morning, Whitby' (pl.39) and his fine watercolour 'Robin Hood's Bay' (untraced) date from this period. So too does his masterly etching touched with drypoint 'The Five Sisters, York Minster' (R.397,pl.40)[16], which rightly ranks as one of his best. In its dimensions, composition and tone this etching captures wonderfully the vast height and space of the cathedral, the grace and beauty of the great window in the north transept, consisting of five huge lancets filled with 13th century glass, each over fifty feet in height and five feet wide, with five smaller lancets with modern glass above, and the play of light from the unseen east windows. In its variations of tone it is suggestive of colour just as much as of light and shadows. Only 30 impressions were pulled, the plate being worked on frequently as printing progressed. It sold for eight guineas, most going to American collectors, of which there were a growing number. 'The Five Sisters', as it is usually called, is one of his best known etchings and was sought avidly by collectors in the halcyon days for prints of the 1920s. In 1923 an impression sold at auction for £370 and in 1929 one made an auction record of £640 (equivalent to around £15,500 today). This was more than Cameron received for some of his oils at that time. It is also interesting to note that then collectors valued an etching more highly than the original drawing. However, the Depression ended the etching boom of the previous thirty years and by 1936 its auction price had fallen to £162 15s., still a very substantial price measured in today's terms.[17]

Cameron's growing reputation as a painter and etcher was acknowledged in his election to membership of some of the principal exhibiting bodies. He was made an Associate of the International in 1901. On 16th March, 1904 he was elected an Associate of the RSA at the sixth attempt, polling 30 votes. The other successful candidates were Robert Brough and John Campbell Mitchell, who polled 24 votes each. Cameron had been nominated for election for the first time in 1893 along with 55 other hopefuls for the three vacancies, including Thomas Millie Dow, E. A. Hornel, W. Y. Macgregor, James Paterson and Alexander Roche. Cameron failed to get any votes on that occasion, but he tried again in 1896, 1901, 1902 and 1903.[18] This was quite normal – aspiring Associates had to work their way up the lists. He was elected to membership of the English and Scottish watercolour societies in 1904 and 1906 respectively, serving on the Council of the RSW from 1907 to 1909 and from 1916 to 1918.

Cameron's stature as an etcher and painter was being recognised also in some of the principal centres for art on the Continent. Along with Axel Haig, William Nicholson and Frank Short, he was awarded a first-class gold medal for etching at the Exposition Universelle Internationale in Paris in 1900; he also received an 'Honourable Mention' for his oil painting 'The Avenue'. He had shown 'The Bride' at the second exhibition of the Berlin

PLATE 39 (OPPOSITE)
Early Morning, Whitby c.1906
Oil on canvas, 36 × 24
Duncan R. Miller Fine Arts

PLATE 40 (ABOVE)
The Five Sisters, York Minster 1907
Etching touched with drypoint (state II)
15⅜ × 7¼
Garton & Co

Secession in 1900 and the same year was elected an Extraordinary Corresponding Member of the Secession. Shortly afterwards he was made a Corresponding Member of the Munich Secession and in 1905 he was awarded a gold medal at Munich's Internationale Kunstausstellung.

1 The Art Journal, 1901, p.62
2 The Art Journal, 1903, p.59
3 The Art Journal, 1902, p.92
4 The Art Journal, 1903, p.59
5 Sir Francis Newbolt, History of the Royal Society of Painter-Etchers & Engravers, Print Collectors' Club No.9, 1930, p.46
6 Frederick Wedmore, Cameron's Etchings, R. Gutekunst, London, 1903
7 Sir James Caw, 'Sir D. Y. Cameron', Old Watercolour Society Club Vol. 27, 1949, p.4
8 Watt
9 Florence Robertson Cameron, 'The Gospel of D. Y. Cameron – A Personal Memory', The British Weekly, 8th July 1965
10 Letter to The Times dated 22nd September 1945
11 Watt
12 Letter from Cameron to James Connell, Glasgow dated 18th December 1903 (NLS ACC7797.1)
13 Letter from Cameron to James Connell, Glasgow dated 5th January 1906 (NLS ACC7797.1)
14 Letter from Cameron to James Connell, Glasgow dated 8th February 1906 (NLS ACC7797.1)
15 Letter from Cameron to James Connell, Glasgow dated 17th May 1902 (NLS ACC7797.1)
16 Plate 40 illustrates the second (incomplete) state of four. Like most etchers Cameron pulled a few proofs at various stages in the production of a plate in order to check progress. In its final state the space under the roof of the cathedral is in dark shadow, the foreground has been darkened and clustered columns to the extreme right and left are defined.
17 From the records of Christopher Mendez, London
18 Minute Books of the General Assembly of the RSA, Edinburgh

CHAPTER SIX

ONE OF 'THE IMMORTALS'

KATHARINE CAMERON NEVER HAD ANY THOUGHTS OF BEING anything other than an artist. At the age of 85 she told Tom Honeyman, a former Director of Glasgow Art Gallery, who was writing an article about her:

> 'I began life as an artist. It never entered my head not to be an artist. From infancy it was my work and play and at all times I was encouraged by the sympathy and loving interest of my family. Among the recollections is that of being constantly absorbed in drawing and in cutting out little figures to paint them in colour – back and front.'[1]

At her death in 1965 an envelope containing some of those coloured figures was found among her papers.

She inherited her artistic abilities from her mother, who, as has been noted, painted flowers in watercolour. As a youngster the example and encouragement of her mother and particularly of her eldest brother must have been of great benefit to her. Katharine and D. Y. were very close. Their mother had a very busy life; not only did she have a family of seven to bring up, but also she had to carry out the many duties of a minister's wife, which were quite onerous. D. Y., who was almost nine years older than Katharine, took a hand in bringing her up and a very deep bond was forged between them.[2] This close relationship lasted until D. Y.'s marriage in 1896. Thereafter he continued to take a keen interest in what she was doing and helped her when he could. For instance, he arranged for H. C. Marillier, a well-known writer on art matters, to write the introduction to the catalogue for her first one-woman show held in 1900 at the Glasgow gallery of James Connell & Sons (D. Y.'s agents).[3] Later there was some bad feeling between them from time to time, which may have been due to the dim view D. Y. took of Katharine's early close friendship with Arthur Kay, a married man, or it may have had something to do with money, which, like illness, was not a suitable subject for discussion in Cameron circles. However, brother and sister became close again in the 1930s.

Katharine followed her brother to Glasgow School of Art, enrolling for classes in 1889, when she was 15. The students were fortunate in having Fra Newbery as Director. Newbery was born in Devon and came to Glasgow in 1885 at the age of 31, after a period on the teaching staff of the South Kensington Schools in London. A fine painter, Newbery was an enthusiastic and enlightened teacher, who made a significant impact on art education, giving equal encouragement to men and women students. He established Technical Art Studios within the School, adding a number of craft subjects to the curriculum, such as wood carving, metalwork, needlework, book-binding, pottery painting and stained glass. He emphasised both art and design and stressed the importance of practical applications of design. He is regarded as an important catalyst of the Glasgow Style of Art Nouveau, which flourished from around 1894 until the First World War and put Glasgow and Glasgow School of Art firmly on the international map.

Her progress is charted in the School's Annual Reports, which record the grades gained by students in the various class examinations. In her first year (1889-90) she obtained 2nd Class awards in Freehand Drawing and Model Drawing. The following year she got a 2nd Class award in Advanced Plant Drawing in Outline and in the Local Competition that year won a 2nd prize of seven shillings and sixpence for a set of flowers painted in tempera, the external examiners for the latter being the painters Joseph Henderson and James Paterson. She received a 2nd Class award in Advanced Drawing from the Antique in her third year. Katharine performed very well in the examinations in her fourth year (1892-93), obtaining four 1st Class awards – Advanced Model Drawing, Advanced Drawing in Light and Shade, Drawing from the Antique and Elementary Modelling – and two 2nd Class awards – the Honours stage of Design and Painting in Monochrome. Her fellow students in the Honours Design class included Charles Rennie Mackintosh and Frances Macdonald, who obtained 1st Class awards, and Francis Dodd, Herbert MacNair and John Quinton Pringle, who like Katharine got 2nd Class awards.

Katharine was a member of a small circle of female students who called themselves 'The Immortals' – why they chose that title is unknown, although several possible explanations have been suggested.[4] The other members of the group were Janet Aitken (1873-1941), Jessie Keppie (1868-1951), the sister of the architect John Keppie, the sisters Margaret (1864-1933) and Frances Macdonald (1873-1921), who were to marry Charles Rennie Mackintosh and Herbert MacNair respectively, and Agnes Raeburn (1872-1955). Cameron and Raeburn, both painters of landscapes and flowers in watercolour, were to remain close friends until Raeburn's death in 1955.

When John Keppie and Charles Rennie Mackintosh were preparing competitive architectural designs, they frequently worked at Keppie's home in Ayr. Very often Herbert MacNair, who like Mackintosh was employed by the architectural partnership of John Honeyman and Keppie, was there as well. Jessie Keppie, at that time engaged to be married to Mackintosh, would descend on her brother at weekends along with the other 'Immortals'. The girls stayed in two bungalows at nearby Dunure, which were christened 'The Roaring Camp'.[5] The name suggests that everyone had a great time. Certainly it must have been an exciting, as well as a stimulating, experience for the girls, escaping from their families in Glasgow to relative freedom in the company of like-minded souls.

'The Immortals' and their friends contributed to *The Magazine*, a student compilation handwritten by the 'editress' Lucy Raeburn, the sister of Agnes Raeburn. The first volume appeared in November 1893 and there were three further issues up to early 1896. *The Magazine* contained original poetry and prose, mostly in the nature of fable, as well as articles and original watercolours and drawings.[6] The tone of *The Magazine* is rather light-hearted — almost juvenile. Work by Katharine appeared in all four issues — illustrations (including a delicate pen drawing of 'Swend the Swineherd' in a romantic idiom characteristic of her later book illustrations and a tiny end-piece in pen and ink of three pigs' heads with their tails tied together, illustrating a 'silly' article about pigs), a watercolour sketch of hens, and two series of humorous drawings (one depicting two ladies in huge velvet hats, before and after rain, and the other seven sketches of a girl attempting to catch butterflies). Her brother contributed a rough ink drawing of a crest and motto 'Labor omnia vincit improbus' to the third issue and James Craig Annan wrote an article on their visit to Holland in 1892 with several of the photographs taken on their Dutch and Italian journeys pasted into the third and fourth issues.

Lucy Raeburn herself contributed to the first issue an entertaining, if somewhat too clever, preview of work to be shown at the exhibition in November 1893 of the Glasgow School of Art Club, which Fra Newbery had established as an exhibiting society for present and former students of the School. Commenting on Katharine's watercolours, Lucy wrote:

> 'Her chef-d'oeuvre is a very lovely group of pansies, masterly execution, low in key, and very atmospheric; effect upon me — silence — a vision of flower shows, pink tickets, 1st prize, variegated species. I'm told everything she does is right of course, but are these said pansies not a little too ostentatiously perfect, for this wicked world — too good to be interesting? She has a one figure sea-piece, which in its unfinished condition, promises to become a realisation of a poet's dream'. [7]

However, the principal interest in *The Magazine* today lies in its very early watercolours and designs by Mackintosh and the Macdonald sisters. Fra Newbery had introduced Mackintosh and Herbert MacNair, who were both attending evening classes at Glasgow School of Art, to the Macdonald sisters and they became known as 'The Four'. Margaret Macdonald's watercolour 'November 5th', Frances Macdonald's 'A Pond' (both 1894) and Mackintosh's 'Winter' (1895), which all appear in *The Magazine*, are early examples of the stylised drawing which they adopted, many depicting a geometric representation of bulb and bud, leaf and petal — their stylised 'cabbage' rose becoming the symbol of the Glasgow Style — or a melancholy dream world peopled by gaunt, elongated female forms with flowing hair. The grotesque stylisation of some of their figures earned them the sobriquet 'Spook School'. The Four reworked each other's ideas, developing a unique design style in a variety of forms, which was taken up to a greater or lesser extent by a large number of designers in a range of disciplines. Although it was received with less than enthusiasm in either Glasgow or London, the Glasgow Style was acclaimed throughout Continental Europe, particularly in Vienna, Berlin and Turin, around the turn of the century.

The other Immortals were exposed to the same forces which shaped the art of the Macdonald sisters, but their work did not approach the dynamic extreme of the sisters. A number of influences can be discerned in the work of Katharine and her fellow students. The art of the Pre-Raphaelites — particularly that of Rossetti and Burne-Jones — was an important factor. It seems likely that they would have seen their work in the important Pre-Raphaelite collection of the Boyd family at Penkill Castle near Girvan, only a few miles from Dunure.[8] The two beautifully-attired female figures in Katharine's watercolour 'There Were Two Sisters Sat in a Bower, Binnorie O Binnorie' (pl.42) – an updated illustration based on the old Scottish ballad 'The Cruel Sister' – are somewhat similar to Burne-Jones's 'Sidonia von Bork' (indeed in the ballad the elder sister is just as vicious as von Bork – she drowns her younger sister for the love of a knight). Burne-Jones's watercolour was exhibited for the first time at the New Gallery in London in 1892. The influence of Aubrey Beardsley (without his malignancy) and of the Dutch symbolist Jan Toorop, both of whom were featured in *The Studio* in its first issues in 1893, can also be seen, particularly in the work of the Macdonald sisters. Japanese art and the Japanese print also had a marked effect. Some of Katharine's flower studies are very similar to Hokusai's woodblocks of flowers, such as his 'Bell-Flower and Dragonfly' of 1832.[9] Another potent force was the Celtic Revival – an upsurge in interest in Celtic art and in Scottish folk-tales and tradition – which was well underway in both Glasgow and Edinburgh at that time. This influence can be seen clearly in the oil painting 'The Druids: Bringing in the Mistletoe'

(1890, Kelvingrove, Glasgow) by George Henry and E. A. Hornel. But it can also be found in the fondness of the Immortals and some of their fellow students, such as Jessie King (1875-1949), for illustrating Scottish folktales and ballads. The influence of Matthijs Maris can be detected in Katharine's work, for example 'Eileen Alannah' (*c.*1900, pl.43), as well as in that of her brother. She met Maris on several occasions.

Katharine worked in watercolour all her life. She seems to have eschewed oil paint, although it would be strange if she had not tried it at one time or another, particularly as she had a brother who worked extensively in the medium.[10] Her early paintings are predominantly flower pieces, but she also executed a number of romantic figure studies, illustrating characters or incidents from Scottish ballads and folklore. She exhibited her work for the first time in 1891, showing 'September Flowers', priced £3, at the RGI. Over the next 74 years until her death in 1965 she was to submit work to all but three of the Institute's annual exhibitions.

Around 1893 Katharine, together with Janet Aitken, Agnes Raeburn and several other women artists, were elected Members of The Glasgow Society of Lady Artists.[11] Founded in 1882, the Society was probably the first women's art society in Britain and became an important element in the artistic life of the city. The year Katharine joined, the Society had formed itself into a club, taking a lease of 5 Blythswood Square and becoming the first women's club in Scotland, the equivalent of Glasgow Art Club, which did not admit lady members. At that time the women's movement in

PLATE 44
Roses 1894
Watercolour, 21 x 15¼
Private Collection

Scotland was in its infancy and it was regarded as 'rather daring and fast' to be a member. As well as exhibitions of members' work, well-known artists, who later included Katharine's brother and John Lavery, were invited, no doubt to offer helpful criticism. Formal lectures also were held.[12] In order to raise money to buy the property a 'Fancy Fair' was organised in 1895. By all accounts it was a great social event in Glasgow. Held in the Fine Art Galleries in Sauchiehall Street, it lasted four days and raised the staggering sum of £2,777. 3s. 7d – the equivalent of £165,000 today. There were many stalls and various entertainments, such as tableaux vivants organised and designed by artist members. Katharine was one of several of the Immortals who painted scenery for a series of nursery rhymes, as well as acting in them. Mackintosh acted as stage manager, tapping with a stick 'in true French fashion' when the curtain was to be drawn.[13]

Katharine was then 21 – pretty and petite. Her friend Anna Buchan wrote in her autobiography:

'Her large brown eyes seemed full of Celtic melancholy, but she was really the gayest of creatures, and had moments of being wildly funny .... Believing all things and hoping all things, she was an incorrigible optimist. Once whan I was staying with her in the country she rushed into my room at 4am on May-day, shouting: 'Get up, Nan, and let's go out and wash our faces in May dew and we'll be beautiful all the year.' That the charm did not work depressed her not at all.'[14]

Anna Buchan recalled that she had a charming taste in dress. Her clothes were never 'arty', but were always a little different and seemed just right for her.

Katharine and her youngest sister Ruby were devoted to each other. The two girls were vivacious and flirtatious. There were plenty of eligible young men around, whether young assistant ministers attached to their father's church for a short period or family friends, and there was a lot of falling in and out of love.[15]

By this time Katharine had achieved considerable maturity in her watercolours of flowers in terms of technique and composition. 'Roses' (1894, pl.44), painted when she was only twenty, and 'Roses in a Vase' (1895, pl.45) are fine examples – well composed, good drawing, sensitive colour, confident handling. She began to exhibit her work more widely. In 1893 she showed for the first time at the RSW, becoming a regular exhibitor. She exhibited one watercolour 'Joy' at the RSA in 1894, but did not show again until 1901. In company with her brother she contributed two somewhat unremarkable watercolours – 'Babies and Brambles' and 'The Black Cockade' – to the *Yellow Book* in 1896 and 1897 respectively.

In 1897 she was elected a member of the RSW, a remarkable achievement for a woman who was just a few days away from her twenty-third birthday. Proposed by Glasgow Boy James Paterson and seconded by the veteran John Smart, who had been a pupil and friend of Horatio McCulloch, Katharine had come top of the poll. The same year she had a joint exhibition with her brother at the gallery of Richard Gutekunst in London. She showed seventeen works in watercolour or pencil – delicate

flower drawings, two figure studies and three or four studies of bees, a creature which became a firm favourite with her and appeared in many of her paintings and etchings almost to the point of superfluity. With the exception of her figure studies, on which one critic commented 'she seems to struggle laboriously after an effect'[16], the exhibition was well received. The correspondent of the *Glasgow Herald* wrote:

> 'Miss Cameron has modelled herself – wisely as it proves – on the Japanese method of arranging flowers for painting, of selecting and throwing her branch or spray of flowers across her paper. Then her sympathy with the flowers is very keen, her touch light and suggestive, and I have rarely seen anything more beautiful in pencil drawing than her hovering bumble bees …'[17]

It appears that early in 1898 Katharine visited Italy. No details survive of where she went or who accompanied her. It seems rather unlikely that she went on her own. There is nothing to suggest that her brother and his wife went to Italy that year and she may have gone with one or more of her fellow students. She later tended to be hazy about dates and events. No information can be gleaned from the lists of work exhibited over the following few years and nothing with an Italian flavour appears to have survived (although she was to illustrate Amy Steedman's *Legends and Stories of Italy for Children* published in 1909). The only clues are contained in an unidentified press cutting of 1898 in the family papers '… she has gone to Italy to prosecute her art' and in the article by H. C. Marillier in *The Art Journal* in 1900 '… her training has been chiefly in Glasgow and Italy'.

In 1898 Katharine tried something new. She executed her first etching 'Wild Bees', an impression measuring some eight inches by two inches. The plate was forgotten about until 1928, when it was found by her brother, which suggests that the proofs were printed on his press. With a brother who was establishing a name for himself as an etcher of considerable promise, she must have been familiar with the etching process and it is only to be expected that she would try it for herself. However, she did not take up the etching needle again until 1909, when she executed a further two plates, 'April' and 'The Tryst', both of bees and blackthorn blossom.

The Rev. Robert Cameron had resigned the charge of Cambridge Street Church in November 1897. Sadly he did not enjoy his retirement for very long, dying the following April at the age of 72. This meant that his widow, along with Joanna and Katharine, had to vacate the manse at 10 South Park Terrace – Ruby had already left home the previous year to act as housekeeper to her brother James, who was minister of the United Presbyterian church at Craigs and Duntocher to the north-west of Glasgow. The women decided to leave Glasgow for Stirling, moving into a house at 19 Victoria Square in 1900, around the same time that D. Y. and his wife moved from London to Kippen, which is only a few miles from Stirling.

Katharine's first one-woman show was held at the Glasgow galleries of James Connell & Sons, opening in December 1900. It had been planned to have the exhibition earlier, but it had to be postponed due to 'the restlessness caused by the [South African] War'.[18] Her brother was anxious that her first solo exhibition should be a success and helped her prepare for

PLATE 45
Roses in a Vase *1895*
Watercolour, 21½ x 12½
Rachel Moss

it. She wrote to Connells towards the end of 1899:

> 'Mr. Harry Marrillier [sic] of London is passing through Glasgow next week & is coming to my studio to see my work before writing the introduction to the Catalogue. Could I trouble you to send it out? I should like to show it to him here, in my studio, as he wants to make a careful study of it, & my brother will be here to explain it all.[19]

The exhibition was representative of her work to date – flowers, figure studies illustrating ballads, fantastic fairies and goblins, and the ubiquitous bees. It received good reviews, the critic of *The Artist* commenting:

> 'It is a little show that no lover of art ought to miss, for rarely have we come across so exquisite a combination of imaginative invention and technical skill. Miss Cameron has hitherto only been known as a remarkably clever painter of flowers; this time she has made an excursion into the realm of fancy.[20]

An article on Katharine by H. C. Marillier appeared in *The Art Journal* in 1900. He wrote:

> '... She has the true race feeling of the Celt for love and legend ... Old ballads and fairy mysteries furnish most of her themes in this class of work, and the direct simplicity of her painting, her skilful drawing and composition, and rich feeling for colour, are all in accord to give added excellence to her most successful pictures'.[21]

The show also included several portrait miniatures. Katharine exhibited miniatures of her sister Ruby and of Anna Buchan at the annual exhibition of the RSA the following year.

Katharine appears to have continued to attend Glasgow School of Art on and off until 1901. She is recorded as being a student in 1894-95, 1899-1900 and 1900-01, although she is not mentioned in the class awards in the School's Annual Reports for those years. However, it seems that this was fairly common practice for female students. Janet Aitken and Agnes Raeburn both enrolled in 1887 and continued at the School until 1901 and 1902 respectively; Jessie Keppie was a student from 1889 to 1900.

Katharine also studied at the Academie Colarossi in Paris. Details of when she went to Paris and how long she stayed are not recorded. However, it is documented that after her return from Paris she was asked to do book illustrations. Her first commission was the illustrations for Louey Chisholm's *In Fairyland*, which was published in 1904. Also, in one of her notebooks is a tiny sketch of a gendarme, inscribed in her hand 'The 1st thing we saw on the pier at Calais. April 1st 1902'.[22] Therefore, it seems safe to assume that she went to Paris in 1902. Another Immortal Janet Aitken attended Colarossi's the same year, so that it is probable that the two girls went to Paris together. D. Y. Cameron and his wife also visited Paris that year, but did not arrive until May.[23]

A period of training in Paris was regarded as a valuable experience for a budding artist. Arthur Melville had advised F. C. B. Cadell to go to Paris, when Cadell became disillusioned with the training in Edinburgh. Paris was the cultural centre of Europe, its lively artistic life acting as a magnet for artists from many countries, thronging the studios, streets and cafes of Montparnasse. When Katharine was there Cezanne was still alive and Matisse had not yet sparked off the Fauvist movement.

The Academie Colarossi in the Rue de la Grande Chaumiere was one of the leading teaching ateliers. Life drawing classes were its central activity and it attracted many foreign students. Both S. J. Peploe and J. D. Fergusson had attended classes there in the mid-1890s. Women students were accepted on equal terms with men. The 'Glasgow Girls' Bessie Mac-Nicol and Stansmore Dean, who became the second wife of Glasgow Boy Robert Macaulay Stevenson, were former students. However, MacNicol 'found the teaching too repressive'[24] and Fergusson thought it uninspiring and rarely attended, preferring to get on with 'real' painting on his own. What Katharine thought of her time in Paris is not recorded. Certainly it does not appear to have had much effect on her work, but she may have been there for too short a time or may have found neither the subject matter nor the teaching to her liking. The major benefits for most artists lay outside the academies in the galleries and the rich artistic life of the city. The life of an art student in Paris in those days was described by Clive Holland in an article in *The Studio* and he went on to say:

> 'The rivalry of a school like Colarossi's is keen and helpful, the discussions which take place when the light has grown dim, and the day's work is over in the studios, or later on in the evening … are worth hours of debate of a more academic sort, are more suggestive than mere teaching, more inspiring than the perusal of biographies of successful artists'.[25]

At Colarossi's Katharine met fellow student Hester Frood (1882-1971) from Topsham near Exeter. They must have become friends, because Frood was invited to Scotland. She became a pupil of D. Y. Cameron, the only known instance of Cameron accepting a pupil. A watercolourist and etcher, Frood's landscapes show the strong influence of Cameron.

[1] T. J. Honeyman, 'Katharine Cameron', *Scottish Field*, October 1959, p.26

[2] Watt

[3] Letter from D. Y. Cameron to James Connell & Sons dated 24 May 1899 (NLS ACC7797.1)

[4] See Jude Burkhauser, 'The 'Girls' of Roaring Camp: 'The Immortals'', article in *Glasgow Girls*, Edinburgh, 1990, p.50

[5] Thomas Howarth, *Charles Rennie Mackintosh and the Modern Movement*, London, 1977, p.58

[6] Katharine Cameron gifted the only known copy of the four issues to Glasgow School of Art in 1949 '… in memory of very interesting and wonderful days at the Glasgow School of Art when we were all there, working very hard in – I can't remember what year – so long ago … !!'

[7] *The Magazine*, first issue November 1893, Glasgow School of Art

[8] Katharine's brother James married Florence Evelyn Cortis-Stanford, whose mother was a Boyd, but they did not meet until 1895 and were kept apart for a decade

[9] *Hokusai* (no.54), Royal Academy, London, 1991

[10] The SSA's 1915 exhibition catalogue lists two oils by Katharine Cameron ('Corfe Castle' and 'Rolington Farm'), but this may be a mistake

[11] The early records of the Society were destroyed by fire in 1898, so that the exact date of Katharine Cameron's election is not known

[12] Ailsa Tanner, *Glasgow Society of Lady Artists*, Centenary Exhibition catalogue, 1982, p.6

[13] DeCourcy Lewthwaite Dewar, *History of The Glasgow Society of Lady Artists' Club*, Glasgow, 1950, p.14

[14] Anna Buchan, *Unforgettable, Unforgotten*, London, 1945, p.85

[15] Watt

[16] *Daily Chronicle*, 26th September 1897

[17] *Glasgow Herald*, 22nd September 1897

[18] Letter from D. Y. Cameron in Venice to James Connell & Sons, Glasgow (no date) (NLS ACC7797.1)

[19] Letter from Katharine Cameron to James Connell & Sons, Glasgow, dated 9th November, 1899 (NLS ACC7797.1)

[20] *The Artist*, III, 1901

[21] H. C. Marillier, 'The Romantic Water-colours of Miss Cameron', *The Art Journal*, 1901, p.149

[22] Album Amicorum of Katharine Cameron (NLS ACC8950.19)

[23] D. Y. Cameron wrote a letter to Connells in Glasgow from Hotel de la Marine, Boulevard Montparnasse, Paris on 6th May 1902 (NLS ACC7797.1)

[24] Ailsa Tanner, Bessie MacNicol, article in *Glasgow Girls*, Edinburgh, 1990, p.193

[25] Clive Holland, 'Student Life in the Quartier Latin, Paris', *The Studio*, Vol.27, 1902, p.33-40

CHAPTER SEVEN

'THE VISIONS OF THE HILLS'

IN 1907 D. Y. CAMERON EXHIBITED 'THE EILDON HILLS' (c.1907, Stirling) at the RGI. The following year at the RSA he showed 'Criffel' (c.1907, Edinburgh City Art Centre), a view across fields to the estuary of the Nith and the mound-shaped hill of Criffel in the background. Both paintings are pure landscape. The absence of any figures marks a departure for Cameron (although he was to continue placing them in some of his architectural paintings). However, of more significance is the fact that Cameron increasingly was turning to the landscape of Scotland for his inspiration.

He was then 42 years of age and well established as an artist. For a number of years his work had received a considerable amount of critical acclaim both at home and abroad. He could sell virtually all he produced. By his election as an Associate of the RSA in 1904 he had been admitted as a member of the Scottish art establishment. In upbringing, temperament, outlook and inclination he was even then the epitome of a pillar of the establishment.

Cameron's landscapes are in the tradition of Scottish landscape painting handed down from Alexander Nasmyth (1758-1840), the Rev. John Thomson of Duddingston (1778-1840) and Horatio McCulloch (1805-1867). After the turn of the century Cameron turned his back on the decorative style of the Glasgow Boys; indeed, he was the only member of that group to

PLATE 46
Cir Mhor *1912*
Oil on canvas, 45¼ × 51¼
Glasgow Art Gallery & Museum

PLATE 47
The Boddin, Angus c.*1911*
Oil on canvas, 29½ × 39½
Flemings

look to the Highlands – the likes of James Paterson and E. A. Walton painted lowland landscapes. Neither did he adopt the impressionistic style of William McTaggart (1835-1910), who was moving towards expressionism during the final decade of his life. Nor did he travel the road to France, taken around the same time by S. J. Peploe (1871-1935) and J. D. Fergusson (1874-1961), who were influenced profoundly by Cezanne, Matisse and the Fauves. At this stage Cameron was closer to the style of Sir George Reid and the late George Paul Chalmers and the palette of William Nicholson, James Pryde and W. R. Sickert.

By about 1910 Cameron had developed an individual landscape style, which was to change little over the next thirty-five years, although his palette went through a number of phases, ranging from sombre browns, greys and black to unrestrained blue, plum, pink, gold and red. He had assimilated certain elements of the style of the Scottish landscape painters of the past, particularly a sense of order and balance – a clarity of landscape – derived from Nasmyth and David Roberts. Cameron's oil painting was always controlled and refined; he rarely let himself go or reached for something beyond his grasp. He never adopted the freedom of handling of Thomson, although he was to embrace Thomson's breadth of treatment. One only has to look at Cameron's paintings of the rugged mountains of Arran, such as 'Cir Mhor' (1912, pl.46), to appreciate that he could be just as dramatic in his treatment of subject matter as Thomson, though in a more subtle manner. Similarly, he was just as interested as McCulloch in portraying the beauty and grandeur of the Scottish Highlands, but he achieved that through design and the use of colour, rather than through picturesque detail. In his realistic treatment of landscape Cameron had assimilated also something of the style of Corot and the artists of the Barbizon and Hague Schools, whom he admired so much.

Cameron had an acute sense of design in terms of structure, tone and balance, which was derived from his etching. He used a strong line to build up the structure of a landscape. He accentuated mass and tonal relationships, the balance between light and shadow. He tended to eliminate everything trivial or inconsequential, which gave many of his landscapes an austere beauty. Although his palette had lightened somewhat from the dark tones of four or five years before, his colour was still rather subdued – cool greens, yellows, browns, greys and blues predominate with the occasional passage in a dull orange or red. 'Criffel' and 'Isles of the Sea' (*c*.1909, Walker, Liverpool) are typical landscapes of the period. This use of restrained colour was to continue until about 1915 or 1916, when occasionally he would employ much richer colour, though still somewhat dark in tone, as in the dramatic 'Balquhidder' (*c*.1916, Laing, Newcastle).

PLATE 48
The Marble Quarry,
Island of Iona *1909*
Oil on canvas, 40⅜ × 50½
Bradford City Art Gallery

PLATE 49
The Peaks of Arran c.1912
Crayon and watercolour, 13 × 19½
Flemings

His handling of paint too was restrained, except on the few occasions when he did let himself go and adopted what was for him a much freer style, as in 'The Marble Quarry, Island of Iona' (1909, pl.48) and 'The Boddin, Angus' (c.1911, pl.47), both of which must rank among his best works.

His was a very personal vision of the varied landscape of Scotland. His intense love for Scotland and its scenery are immediately apparent in his paintings. He was a Romantic and had inherited from Thomson and McCulloch the sense of association of Scotland's landscape with its history and literature, which was heightened by a feeling that, through Clan Cameron and his 'family ties' with Archibald Cameron, he was part of Scotland's history. In 1926 he wrote from Achnasheen in Ross-shire to (Sir) Evelyn Shaw, the London Secretary of the British School at Rome:

'Would that you could see this amazing County – one for Millais or for Blake. I think the Psalmist must have known it, & its towering mountains & profound lochs. I have been deep in books of the last risings of the Stuarts, in which my people were much engaged & suffered incredibly.'[1]

He sought to convey the spirit of place. An address he gave in 1928 on 'The Romance of Scottish History' is revealing as an indication of what he was trying to achieve:

'Romance in history as in the arts was that spell of mystic beauty, haunted by strangeness of form and colour, remote from the facts and feelings of common life. It did not imply lack of strength but associated itself with very noble, exalted, and even austere shapes, veiled perhaps by distance or muted by the fading light and gathering darkness. Out of these shadows of the centuries, often profound in colour and strangely lit, there emerged great figures or actions which they associated with the world of romance. The rhythm in poetry rather than prose, the tones and colours in painting rather than the forms in sculpture, were more expressive of these visions of the dream world of beauty and mystery they longed for in a life where pressure of the actual hindered the imaginative impulses which fired and exalted the heart'.[2]

This personal vision of the romance and inter-relationship of history and art goes a long way in helping us to understand Cameron's work, particularly his late landscapes.

The words of the poet Wordsworth, which Cameron quoted in a speech in 1932 to commemorate the Centenary of the death of that arch-Romantic Sir Walter Scott, seem to encapsulate the essence of his work in landscape:

'the visions of the hills
  and souls of lonely places'[3]

Like Thomson, Cameron strove to communicate the breadth and beauty of the Scottish landscape, both on a spiritual and an artistic level. What lover of Scotland can fail to be moved by the stark beauty of 'The Hill of the Winds' (c.1913, pl.50), the tranquil peace of evening in 'The Tweed' (c.1905, pl.51), the dark, brooding 'Peaks of Arran' (c.1912, pl.49) or the sheer romance and dramatic effect of 'The Boddin, Angus' (pl.47)? The latter depicts not some ancient temple on the Nile, but a lowly lime kiln on

PLATE 50
The Hill of the Winds c.1913
Oil on canvas, 46 × 52½
National Gallery of Scotland

PLATE 51 (LEFT)
The Tweed c.*1905*
Watercolour, 10¼ × 16¼
Flemings

PLATE 52 (BELOW)
Old Cairo *1908*
Watercolour over pencil, 17½ × 8
Flemings

the Angus coast about to be engulfed by a dark storm. Although often occupied with other work, Cameron was to return to painting the landscape of Scotland whenever he could throughout the rest of his life.

Cameron also turned from time to time to his other great love – architecture. In 'South Aisle, Tewkesbury' (*c.*1908, untraced), which was exhibited at the RSA in 1908, Cameron demonstrates his mastery of cathedral architecture – the mass and mystery of a complex pattern of lofty columns, arches and windows, which borders on the abstract. It was executed as an etching (R.457) in 1915 and exhibited the same year at the RA in London. 'Craigievar' (pl.54) was exhibited at the RSA in 1909. *The Art Journal* considered that the painting conformed to the definition of architecture as 'music breathed into space'.[4] Within an imaginative design Cameron has not only captured the great mass of the castle, but also enhanced its fairy-tale quality. The castle was completed in 1626 for William Forbes, who had made a fortune from his dealings in the Baltic port of Danzig, which earned him the nicknames 'Danzig Willie' and 'Willie the Merchant'.

The Camerons wintered in Egypt in 1908-9, staying in Cairo and visiting the city's museums, the Pyramids at Giza and the other historical sites in and around Cairo. They also made the journey of over 400 miles to the southern city of Luxor to see the vast ruins of the ancient Egyptian capital of Thebes. Cameron executed many drawings on their travels, such as 'Old Cairo' (1908, pl.52). Those he worked up into several oil paintings, as well as a number of etchings such as 'The Turkish Fort' (R.409), a fortification in the Muqattam Hills overlooking Cairo, and 'The Desert' (R.410), a fragment of one of the Pyramids at Giza. The reviewer of an exhibition of contemporary art at the Goupil Gallery in 1909 praised his oil painting 'The Citadel, Cairo' (1909, untraced), remarking that work by Cameron, William Orpen and William Nicholson formed the high point of the show.[5] At the RSA in 1910 he exhibited the impressive 'Nightfall, Luxor' (1909, Walker, Liverpool). In its subject matter and very dark blue tones, it is a

very dramatic – almost theatrical – painting; the last glow of sunset just above the opposite bank of the Nile is seen from between two immense columns of the Temple of Luxor.

From the lists of works exhibited by Cameron it appears that they may have returned to France in 1910, visiting Amiens, Beauvais, Chartres and Paris. The impressive architectural view 'Old Paris' (pl.55) was exhibited at the RSA in 1911, though in style and tone it could date from five or six years earlier. Certainly his etchings 'Beauvais' (R.412, pl.53), 'The Chimera of Amiens' (R.415) and 'The Wingless Chimera' (R.416) date from 1910-11. The latter two etchings of stone gargoyles – so finely drawn – caused much discussion among collectors.

Cameron's etchings featured regularly in exhibitions, many mounted by his agent James Connell in either London or Glasgow. In 1909 Cameron and his younger fellow etcher Muirhead Bone had been included with the 'Masters' – Rembrandt, Durer, Whistler, Meryon and Haden – in an exhibition at the galleries of Obach & Co. in London. American collectors too were keenly interested in his etchings. In New York the Grolier Club organised an exhibition in 1908. A further exhibition was held at the New York gallery of Arthur H. Hahlo & Co. in 1912. Several substantial collections were built up over time. Etchings from the collection of Mr. E. M. Herr were exhibited at the Carnegie Institute in Pittsburgh in 1919; exhibitions of Cameron's etchings were held by the Institute also in 1911 and 1920. It is somewhat ironic that today one has to travel to the United States to have a reasonable certainty of seeing a particular Cameron print. The Public Library in Boston has well over 400 of the 520 or so which Cameron produced, the gift of the New York collector Albert H. Wiggin. Lessing Rosenwald gifted just under 400 prints and some 50 drawings to the National Gallery of Art in Washington; Cameron etched a book plate (R.489) for Rosenwald and his wife in 1930. The Metropolitan Museum in New York has over 300, mainly the gift of Mr. H. B. Dick, for whom Cameron also etched a book plate (R.423).[6] In Europe the principal collections are held by the British Museum in London and in Berlin, Budapest and Dresden, but these are much smaller than their American counterparts. The Scottish galleries have been adding to their rather meagre holdings in recent years as prints have come up for sale.

Cameron's achievement as one of the foremost etchers of his day was recognised in 1911, when he was made an Associate-Engraver of the RA, filling the vacancy caused by the promotion of the etcher Frank Short to full Academician. Five years later Cameron was elected an Associate-Painter, along with Maurice Greiffenhagen, Head of the Life School at Glasgow School of Art, and Bertram Priestman. Cameron is the only person to have achieved the double distinction of being elected an Associate for engraving and for painting. Indeed, he was one of only three Glasgow Boys to be elected to the RA. George Henry had been made an Associate-Painter in 1907 and John Lavery was elected an Associate-Painter in 1911 on the same day as Cameron. The coincidence was to be repeated in 1920, when both Cameron and Henry were elected full Academicians; Lavery had to wait another year. Cameron was elected to full membership of the RWS, the

PLATE 53
Beauvais *1910*
Etching and drypoint, 10 × 8
Private Collection

PLATE 54
Craigievar *1909*
Oil on canvas, 40 × 22¼
Aberdeen Art Gallery

English watercolour society, second only to the RA in terms of seniority, in 1915.

Turning back to 1911, Cameron received another honour that year, when he was awarded the Honorary Degree of Doctor of Laws by Glasgow University. To a man who had left school at sixteen, this must have brought especial pleasure. The same year Cameron issued what is regarded as one of his finest prints, the etching and drypoint 'Ben Ledi' (R.424, pl.58), which he exhibited at the RA that year. The mountain was a constant source of inspiration for him and he painted it in its varied moods many times. The print expert Harold Wright, who knew him for over forty years, later recalled that Cameron never failed to point out the distant peak to visitors and always spoke of it affectionately and reverently – 'that's Ben Ledi ... very beautiful, isn't it?'[7] The print is rich and full-toned, with dramatic contrasts of light and shade. However, it is too dark for some, who choose the etching and drypoint 'Ben Lomond' (R.468, pl.57), executed in 1923, as Cameron's best landscape print.

Frank Rinder's Catalogue of Cameron's etchings was published in 1912, following a slim introductory volume in 1908. A writer on art matters, Rinder became a close friend of Cameron and he and his wife were frequent visitors to Dun Eaglais until his death in 1937. Rinder issued an enlarged edition of his Catalogue in 1932, when Cameron had all but given up etching. It lists every known state of all his etchings and drypoints and is an essential source of reference for collectors, not to mention a biographer who did not have the benefit of knowing Cameron personally.

In 1914 Cameron was appointed to a Representative Committee which was being set up to consider the establishment of a national collection of modern Scottish art, a project which in various guises was to have a particularly long period of gestation. Thirty years later Cameron was to lament in a foreword to the catalogue of a joint RSW/Scottish Modern Arts Association exhibition that a national gallery of modern art still remained a dream. Other artist members of the committee included Sir James Guthrie, then the President of the RSA, Alexander Roche and E. A. Walton. A

PLATE 57 (OPPOSITE LEFT)
Ben Lomond *1923*
Etching and drypoint, 10¼ × 16¼
Garton & Co

PLATE 58 (OPPOSITE RIGHT)
Ben Ledi *1911*
Etching and drypoint, 14⅞ × 11⅞
The Fine Art Society

PLATE 59 (LEFT)
Stirling Castle c.*1916*
Oil on canvas
Private Collection

PLATE 60 (BELOW)
Stirling Castle c.*1910*
Chalk and wash, 12½ × 14
Private Collection

number of prominent figures made up the lay members. This was the first of a number of public appointments which Cameron was to hold. He was an ideal candidate for such a task, for not only was he highly thought of in an artistic sense, but also he was sound and had an air of distinction and authority. Ironically, his last public appointment was to serve on a small committee set up in 1945 under Lord Linlithgow to examine houses suggested by the Scottish Home Department for a gallery of modern art.

Cameron continued his series of Scottish landscapes with hardly a break. 'Ben Vorlich, Autumn' (c.1913), a view across the broad valley of the Forth to the triple peaks of Ben Venue, Ben Ledi and the distant Ben Vorlich bathed in the evening sun, was purchased by the National Gallery in Melbourne in 1914. 'Ben Ledi, Early Spring' (c.1914), the snow-clad mountain towering above the plain of the Forth, was purchased by the Contemporary Art Society and presented to the Tate Gallery in 1917. Other oils of the period include 'Dunstaffnage' (c.1915, Aberdeen) and 'Watch Tower, Berwick' (c.1916, Kirkcaldy). In etching too he was concentrating mainly on Scottish landscape, producing between 1911 and 1917 a series of drypoints noted for their simple design and wonderful quality of line. It is difficult to choose between them, but 'Dinnet Moor' (R.431), 'The Cairngorms' (R.455) and 'Hills of Tulloch' (R.458) are outstanding.

In 1917 Cameron exhibited three oil paintings of architectural subjects. These included 'Ypres' (pl.62) and 'Rue du Bourg, Chartres' (Tate, London), a finely-observed study of the corner of an old building with an interesting shop front at ground level and a curious turret-like projection at the corner of the upper storey. The sketches for these paintings must have been done several years earlier, as during the First World War it would have been impossible for him to visit Ypres and it seems unlikely that he would have been allowed to travel to Chartres. Although he did go to France, that was not until the end of 1917. Indeed, the style of both paintings is close to that of etchings of similar subjects dated at least ten years earlier (for example, the drypoint 'House Front, Ypres' (R.396A) of 1907-30), which makes dating the two paintings somewhat problematical. However, the studies for the oil painting 'Cafe Leroux' (pl.56), a street

scene in Boulogne, exhibited at the RA in 1918, could have been made when he passed through the port in October 1917.

At the outbreak of war in 1914 Cameron at 49 was much too old to enlist, but he joined the Volunteers at Kippen. However, he did experience life at the front for a short period in 1917. In the second half of that year Cameron, Augustus John and Gyrth Russell were hired by Lord Beaverbrook as war artists, joining four other artists – three Canadians, including A. Y. Jackson, and one Englishman, Richard Jack – to record the exploits of the Canadian Expeditionary Force on the Western Front for the Canadian War Memorials Fund. Devised by the Canadian-born newspaper magnate and Lord Rothermere, the Fund had been established at the end of the previous year. Its aim was to produce a permanent collection of paintings and sketches relating to Canada's contribution to the Allied war effort, whether at the front, in Britain or at home in Canada. By early 1918 about 55 artists – Canadian and British – were involved, of whom roughly half travelled to the war zone. Ultimately around 116 painters and sculptors were associated with the Fund, creating over 800 works of art.[8]

At first only four artists were allowed to go to the front at any one time. They were paid by the Canadian Army according to their rank, kitted out in officer's uniform and billeted at the headquarters of the Canadian War Records Office, which usually was well behind the lines. In addition to a batman, they had a car and driver to take them to and from their chosen sketching locations. Normally an artist was allotted a period at the front ranging from three weeks to about two months, so they had to work fairly quickly, concentrating on sketches in pencil and watercolour. Not surprisingly, they were taken for spies on a number of occasions! Although their quarters were luxurious compared with those in the trenches, conditions were far from ideal. Often they had to sketch in fairly severe weather – the winter of 1917-18 was very cold. There was the noise and confusion of the battle, as well as the ever present danger from shelling, if not from sniper fire or a surprise infantry attack.

Cameron was one of a number of artists who worked under fire.[9] He had agreed to execute two oil paintings for the Fund and went to France around the middle of October 1917 with the rank of Major to do preliminary sketches for one of the paintings.[10] At that time the Canadian troops were at Passchendaele, moving to the Vimy-Lens front in November, where they were to remain until late the following spring.[11] Cameron was due to return to the front that spring, but his journey was postponed at the last moment; in April 1918 he wrote to James Connell, who had enquired about the availability of paintings for sale:

> 'I went to London 3 weeks ago en route to France again, but my departure was postponed owing to this present fighting [?] over the [?] ground I would have been in had I gone 2 days sooner. Now I just await permission. As to pictures I have been so engaged in a very large canvas for the Canadian Government that little else has been possible. I have another very large one to do & probably another war picture at least after that so my time is not my own .... I fear it will be later in the season before I have anything to offer, and when I shall be able to turn to plates I cannot think yet.'[12]

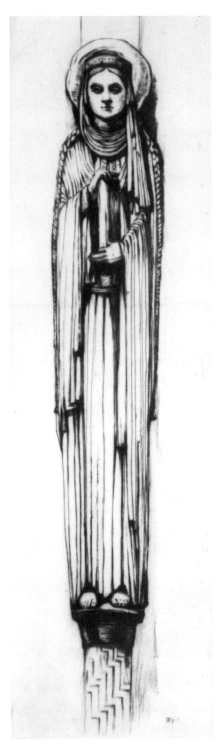

PLATE 61 (ABOVE)
A Queen of Chartres *1912-30*
Drypoint, unfinished, 15¾ × 4⅜
Garton & Co

PLATE 62 (OPPOSITE)
Ypres *c.1906*
Oil on canvas, 36 × 24
Ewan Mundy Fine Art

However, it appears that he did not return to France until January 1919, by which time the war was over and only the devastation remained. On this occasion he sketched in the vicinity of Ypres in south west Belgium. He was looking for material not only for his second Canadian painting, but also for a work he had promised to the British Pictorial Propaganda Committee.

In March 1918 Beaverbrook had been made Chancellor of the Duchy of Lancaster and had joined the War Cabinet in charge of a new Ministry of Information. Cameron was one of an initial group of thirty artists who had been asked by the Ministry to produce a painting relating to the war. He was offered £300 plus the cost of materials, travelling expenses and a subsistence allowance whilst abroad and, if necessary, a special studio for an oil 72 inches high and 125 inches wide. This painting was to be one of a series by distinguished artists, including Colin Gill, John and Paul Nash, William Roberts, John Singer Sargent, who produced a poignant portrayal of a line of blinded soldiers in 'Gassed', and Henry Tonks.[13] Muirhead Bone was in charge of organising the work, which was to be hung in a new Hall of Remembrance. Regrettably the project was never completed and the huge paintings were handed over to the newly established Imperial War Museum.

On returning from his second visit to France, Cameron wrote to Alfred Yockney at the Ministry:

'Yes after much searching & [?] I found my theme twixt Ypres & Menin – really the 'Road to the Front' & am in fond hope I shall be able to make something of

PLATE 63
A Garment of War c.1926
Oil on canvas, 48 × 65¾
Edinburgh City Art Centre

it. I am expecting the canvas any day now & will start my composition at once.'[14]

By November 1919 he had completed the painting and was able to tell Yockney:

'I have decided to call the picture 'The Battlefield of Ypres – After'. It is not a portrait of any one spot (photographers can do all that) but is founded on my notes on the Road from Ypres to Menin...'[15]

Cameron's first painting for the Canadian War Memorials Fund, 'Flanders from Kemmel', was hung at the Fund's exhibition at the RA in January 1919. Similarly, 'The Battlefield of Ypres' (pl.64) was shown at the National War Art Exhibition mounted by the British authorities at the RA at the end of 1919, despite a last minute panic about whether the painting would arrive in time. His second oil for the Canadians is titled 'The Battlefields at Ypres' and is very similar to the painting he executed for the British. In these paintings Cameron adopted his usual approach to landscape painting. Indeed, most of the artists used familiar conventions in their treatment of the scenes they were depicting. This led the art adviser to the British Pictorial Propaganda Committee to remark on 'the monotony of themes ... scarcely half a dozen' and 'a ghastly sameness in treatment, even allowing for different temperament and degrees of merit' when he saw the paintings in the summer of 1918.[16] However, his reaction seems rather

PLATE 64
The Battlefield of Ypres *1919*
Oil on canvas, 72 × 125
Imperial War Museum, London

harsh. The fault lay more in the choice and number of artists. Although there were over 100, most of them were traditionalists and so it was not surprising that their work was so similar. It was only from the younger and more avant-garde artists, such as Sydney Carline, Paul Nash, C. R. W. Nevinson and Percy Wyndham Lewis, that a range of striking images of the war were forthcoming. Perhaps a further answer to the art adviser's criticism is that there was considerable pressure on the artists by the authorities to complete their work in time for the respective exhibitions at the RA. For many artists what they had experienced at the front possibly did not sink in until later. For instance, Cameron's 'A Garment of War' (pl.63), which was not executed until around 1926, when it was exhibited at the RSA, is a far more potent image of the horrors of war than 'The Battlefield of Ypres', although the latter conveys well the desolation and futility of war.

Cameron's war paintings occupied most of his time from October 1917 to almost the end of 1920. In addition to his work for the British and Canadian authorities, he executed a number of other war paintings, including 'Bailleul' (c.1919, pl.65), exhibited at the RSA in 1919 and 'The Ruins of Ypres' (c.1919, Ashmolean, Oxford). The tranquil 'A Village in Normandy' (pl.66) also dates from this period. The reason why Cameron stopped etching in 1917 is that he simply did not have the time to etch – he had so much other work to complete. Periodically, James Connell wrote asking whether he had returned to etching; usually he got a reply along the lines of:

'... If I had etched any plates I would have told you. I have done nothing but when my large war pictures are away I hope to resume my [?] & perhaps do something worthy before I pass amid the Shadows'.[17]

PLATE 65
Bailleul c.1919
Oil on canvas, 39 × 45
Dundee City Art Gallery

PLATE 66
A Village in Normandy c.*1919*
Oil on canvas, 26 x 36½
Private Collection

However, in November 1920 he was able to report to Connell 'all my war pictures at last away & ready for other things.'[18]

Whilst Cameron was engaged on his work for the Canadians, he was elected a full Academician of the RSA on 13th February 1918, along with Edwin Alexander. His Diploma work was 'The Norman Arch' (pl.67), an architectural study of a corner in Winchester Cathedral, which was exhibited at the Academy in 1919. At the end of 1918 he was asked to serve on the RSA's Scottish War Memorials Advisory Sub-committee, which offered general advice on war memorials, as well as help to individual memorial committees. Cameron's interest in architecture made him just the man for the job. He was involved in the design of many memorials, often in conjunction with his friend Eric Bell, the Stirling architect, including Cambusbarron (1920), Kilmarnock (1921), Morvern (1921) and Alexandria (1922).[19]

In 1919 Cameron's close friend Sir James Guthrie retired from the Presidency of the RSA. Patrick Adam, one of the senior Academicians, sounded out his fellow Academicians as to who should take over from Guthrie. Esme Gordon's history of the Academy records that 'there was one obvious choice, who was distinguished equally as artist and man – D. Y. Cameron, whom some considered the only member with the requisite qualifications'.[20] Cameron declined to be nominated, however, writing in his reply:

'The Presidency is an office held in the past by very eminent men who have left high ideals to live and labour for, and examples of whole-hearted devotion also. It is the memory of those things and the many interests and duties I have in the South which lead me very regretfully to ask you and my friends to put my name aside ... I hope and pray that when the time comes for further steps, one will be chosen with the idealism, the ardour and ambition to fill the post which requires all of a man's mind and energy and initiative to maintain the prestige of the R. S. A'.[21]

It is likely that Cameron would have made a good President – a worthy successor to the excellent Guthrie, who like himself was a son of the manse and of whom on his death in 1930 Cameron said in all sincerity:

> 'He did more than anyone who ever served as President over the Institution to establish it on a sound basis for those who should come after him and make it worthy of the Art and Artists of the country.'[22]

Certainly Cameron had the temperament and outlook to be President. Also he had the respect of his fellow Academicians, as well as the necessary standing within the British art establishment to represent and prosecute the interests of the RSA in wider circles. However, he was right in saying that the office required a man who could devote his whole mind to its business. Cameron felt that with all his other responsibilities he could not do that.

Letter from Cameron to Evelyn Shaw, 27th June 1926 (Archives of British School at Rome, London)

[2] Quoted by Sir James Caw in 'Sir D. Y. Cameron', *Old Watercolour Society Club* Vol.27, 1949, p.6

[3] From typescript of speech by Cameron for Sir Walter Scott Centenary, Stirling, 16th September 1932 (NLS ACC8950.29)

[4] *The Art Journal*, 1909, p.187

[5] Ibid., p.380

[6] Harold J. L. Wright, *Etchings and Drypoints of Sir D. Y. Cameron*, Print Collectors' Club No.24, 1947, p.27

[7] Ibid., p.21

[8] Maria Tippett, *Art at the Service of War*, Toronto, 1984

[9] Ibid., p.53

[10] Letter from Cameron to James Connell, Glasgow dated 5th October 1917 (NLS ACC7797.3)

[11] Tippett, op. cit., p.53

[12] Letter from Cameron to James Connell, Glasgow dated 18th April 1918 (NLS ACC7797.3)

[13] Correspondence between Alfred Yockney and Cameron in D. Y. Cameron file, Imperial War Museum, London

[14] Letter from Cameron to Alfred Yockney dated 6th March 1919 (Imperial War Museum)

[15] Letter from Cameron to Alfred Yockney dated 8th November 1919 (Imperial War Museum)

[16] Tippett, op. cit., p.58

[17] Letter from Cameron to James Connell dated 30th July 1919 (NLS ACC7797.3)

[18] Letter from Cameron to James Connell dated 30th November 1920 (NLS ACC7797.3)

[19] The author is indebted to Mr. Gilbert T. Bell of Glasgow for this information

[20] Esme Gordon, *The Royal Scottish Academy 1826-1976*, Edinburgh, 1976, p.194

[21] Ibid., p.194

[22] Ibid., p.182

PLATE 67
The Norman Arch c.1918
Oil on canvas, 35½ x 23½
Royal Scottish Academy
(Diploma painting)

CHAPTER EIGHT

PAINTING AND PUBLIC LIFE

FOR CAMERON THE 1920S WERE CHARACTERISED BY AN increasing involvement in matters of public interest relating to art, either as an adviser or as a trustee. It was also a period during which he produced some of his finest oil paintings, following visits to the south of France and to Italy.

In 1919 he had been appointed as a member of both the Faculty of Painting and the newly-formed Faculty of Engraving of the British School at Rome. It was the beginning of an association with the School which he came to value greatly and which he enjoyed right up to his death.

The School had been established in Rome in 1900 with the twin objects of promoting the study of Roman and Graeco-Roman archaeology and Roman and Italian studies in general. In 1912 its objects were widened to include painting, sculpture and architecture. The principal responsibility of the members of a faculty, who were based in London, was to judge work submitted by competitors for the award of a Rome Scholarship. Each of the fine art faculties awarded a scholarship annually, which in the early 1920s amounted to £250 per annum tenable for three years. The winners occupied purpose-built live-in studios in a building in Rome, originally designed by Lutyens as the British pavilion at the Rome International Exhibition in 1911 and subsequently enlarged by him to house the School. It was an excellent opportunity for artists to explore new ideas in a stimulating environment (provided, that is, the ideas were not too progressive – in 1932 Sir William Rothenstein opined that the Director of the School should be an artist, rather than an archaeologist as had been the case until then, in order to 'look after the studies of painters, sculptors and engravers, especially in these days when all sorts of extreme 'abstract' ideas are about, which settle like microbes in the students' brains…'!)[1]

In both Faculties Cameron was in very good company. In 1920 the Faculty of Painting was chaired by John Singer Sargent. Apart from Cameron, the other members were George Clausen, Sir Arthur Cope, Dermod O'Brien, William Orpen, Charles Ricketts, Charles Shannon and Philip Wilson Steer. The original members of the Faculty of Engraving were Frank Short as chairman, Muirhead Bone, Cameron, Campbell Dodgson, Charles Shannon and William Strang. No less than seven of them either were members of the Society of Twelve or had exhibited with the Society. Cameron was to resign from the Faculty of Engraving in 1929 due to pressure of work – by then he was on so many boards and committees that he found it difficult to give them all adequate attention – but he remained a member of the Faculty of Painting until his death. He took over as chairman on the death of Sargent in 1925, a position he held until 1938.

Colin Gill, unfairly neglected today, was the first Rome Scholar in painting. Others included Thomas Monnington, who was to become

President of the RA as well as a member of the Faculty, and A. K. Lawrence, who also became a member of the Faculty. Both Monnington and Lawrence became close friends of Cameron; Lawrence painted Cameron's portrait (Scottish National Portrait Gallery). The sculptors Barbara Hepworth and Henry Moore spent a short period at the School, both recalling that the experience had an influence on their future work.[2] Cameron took a keen personal interest in the work of the School and its students. He and his wife visited Rome in January 1923. The Minutes of the Faculty record his impressions:

'After spending a month in close association with all the students he had come to the definite conclusion that they needed not so much the constant guidance and supervision of a permanent Art Director as occasional Visits, say once or twice a year, from artists who could stimulate them in their work and could provide a more personal and intimate connection between the Scholars and the Faculties at home.'[3]

Cameron's suggestion was adopted by the School's Council. The following year he was appointed as the first official Visitor to the School and he and his wife spent almost a month with the students in Rome.[4] Clausen and Rothenstein followed Cameron as Visitors in 1925 and 1926 respectively. The Camerons returned to Italy for a third time during the winter of 1927-28, visiting Rome and travelling south as far as Naples.

In a note written after Cameron's death in 1945 Sir Evelyn Shaw recorded the School's debt to Cameron, continuing:

'Indeed all artists, whatever their medium of expression, found in him a friend so long as they revered the great traditions and shunned what he called 'the craze for speed and exhibition sensationalism'.'[5]

Cameron was elected an Academician of the RA in London in January 1920. He was now a full member of both the English and Scottish Academies. Like its sister institution in Scotland the RA was presented with an architectural piece as Cameron's Diploma painting, in this instance 'Durham' (1920) (pl.68). He executed another oil of Durham Cathedral around the same time, which was purchased for the gallery in Adelaide – the gallery already owned 'The Bride' of 1897.

The same year he was appointed by the Prime Minister Lloyd George as a Trustee of the Tate Gallery 'following a decision to provide fuller representation of practising artists on the Tate's Board'.[6] He held this appointment until 1927. He took his duties as a Trustee very seriously and did everything he could to advance the interests of the Tate. An instance of this was the strenuous efforts made by Cameron in 1921 to secure for the gallery and the nation 'Christ in the House of His Father' by John Everett Millais. Portraying the boyhood of Christ, it is the first important religious subject painted by Millais, though it was vilified by the critics for its down-to-earth depiction of the Holy Family, when it was exhibited for the first time at the Royal Academy in 1850. It came on the market in 1921 and after a battle was eventually secured by the Tate for 10,000 guineas. This was due in no small measure to Cameron, who wrote many letters in an

PLATE 68
Durham *1920*
Oil on canvas, 35½ × 29
Royal Academy (Diploma painting)

attempt to enlist support. It is interesting to note from a letter he wrote to James Connell in Glasgow that he thought the former shipowner Sir Frederick Gardiner might give some money, but he was very doubtful whether any money would be forthcoming from William Burrell.[7] Cameron himself managed to raise in one week over £1,000 from several fellow Scots in London.[8] As well as helping to acquire earlier works, whilst a Trustee he played an active part in bringing the collection up to date through the purchase of work by younger artists with whom he could have had little in common.[9]

In December 1920 he was appointed to the Board of Trustees of the National Galleries of Scotland on the retiral of Sir James Guthrie. It was an appointment which was renewed in April 1922 and every five years thereafter until Cameron's death in 1945. His connection with Scotland's national collections was one which he valued highly. Sir James Caw, the Director of the National Galleries from 1907 to 1930, considered Cameron's help invaluable, recalling that:

'... both he and I always looked back with special pleasure on our 'raids' on London, when, after preliminary scouting, we went round together to look at what had turned up'.[10]

Towards the end of 1920 the Camerons bought a house in London at 40 Queen's Road in St. John's Wood. Now that he was a Royal Academician and had a number of other commitments in London, it was essential to have a comfortable base there. It was much preferable to living in hotels, such as Fleming's Hotel in Half Moon Street and Brown's in Albemarle Street, both convenient for the RA, as they had done until then. The Camerons stayed at their London home frequently during the year, particularly each spring and autumn. Indeed, the RSA placed Cameron on the Non-Resident List from 1920 to 1932.[11]

However, Cameron's growing number of public responsibilities, taken in conjunction with his work in the studio, were having an effect on his health. In August 1921 he suffered a serious heart attack and he was ordered by his doctor to take a complete rest over the following four months.[12] When he had recovered his strength sufficiently, the Camerons went to the south of France to continue his convalescence, staying for several weeks in the winter warmth of Valescure, a village above St. Raphael on the coast between St. Tropez and Cannes.[13] Whilst there Cameron must have felt well enough to do some sketching, because over the next year or so he executed a number of oil paintings of the area. The intensity of light in the south of France had the same effect on Cameron as it had on the Scottish Colourists. The paintings are imbued with the brightest colour that Cameron had used so far, exemplified by 'La Rue Annette' (c.1923, pl.69), a scene in St. Raphael, 'A Little Town in Provence' (1922, Fitzwilliam, Cambridge), a rather free treatment of Frejus near St. Raphael, and 'L'Esterels' (c.1923, pl.70), a scene in the mountains behind St. Raphael. Cameron delighted in depicting quiet corners in town and village. 'Barlou' (pl.71) is another fine example. The location of the village is unknown, perhaps Provence, making the date of the painting around 1923. However,

PLATE 69
La Rue Annette *c.1922*
Oil on canvas, 22½ x 16¾
National Gallery of Scotland

PLATE 70
L'Esterels c.1922
Oil on canvas, 13¾ x 18
Private Collection

it may be somewhere in the Alpes Maritimes, which the Camerons visited in 1926.

The heavy load which Cameron had imposed on himself had taken its toll. Certainly that was the view of Charles Aitken, Director of the Tate Gallery from 1911 to 1930, writing to Cameron:

> '... how profoundly grateful I am to you for your immense services to this gallery and British Art. I am afraid it has been done at great sacrifice to yourself and I am grieved at this.'[14]

However, Cameron did not let up. In December 1922 Charles Ricketts and Cameron were invited to join the Committee of the National Art-Collections Fund. Cameron was to serve on the Committee until 1938, when he was made a Life Member in recognition of his services to the Fund; he acted as Vice-Chairman from about 1929 to 1938. On the formation of the Royal Fine Arts Commission in 1924 he was appointed to it as the only painter member.

Cameron took up etching again in 1923. He had not executed a plate for around six years. At first it had been because he had so much other work to do. At the end of 1920 he told James Connell that he hoped that 'the spirit of etching will descend on me once again'.[15] However, after his heart attack in 1921 he had had to give up all work for a period and it was not until 1923 that he felt able to resume etching. For collectors it was well worth the wait, for two of his three plates that year are superb – 'Ben Lomond' (R.468) and 'Thermae of Caracalla' (R.470). He was to continue etching for another nine years, concentrating mainly on Scottish landscapes, such as 'Balquhidder' (R.491, pl.72), but also executing several architectural subjects, such as 'Gloucester' (R.490), a view of the north aisle of the cathedral.

Early in 1924 Cameron's mother, who was 84, fell ill and it became obvious that she would not recover. It was a merciful release when she died

PLATE 71
Barlou c.1922
Oil on canvas, 24 × 20
Private Collection

in April that year at the family home in Edinburgh. Cameron had supported his mother for the 26 years or so that she had been a widow. How proud she would have been that his commitment to British art and its institutions was recognised later that year, when he was knighted by King George V in the Birthday Honours. He had come a long way from that son of the manse who began as a trainee clerk in a Glasgow iron foundry, attending art school in his spare time. Now he was one of the leading members of the British art establishment – a notable artist whose work was purchased almost before it left the easel and whose advice on art matters was widely sought.

The warm colours which Cameron had used in his Provencal paintings of 1922 and 1923 were repeated in a series of paintings of Rome, following their visits in 1923 and 1924 in connection with the British School at Rome. On their return from the first visit Cameron wrote to James Connell:

'… We had a delightful time in Rome & saw much which I hope to turn to account in the coming months'.[16]

Over the next three years he executed a number of major oils of scenes in and around Rome, such as 'Pietros, Rome' (c.1924, pl.73), the 'Baths of Caracalla' (1924, pl.74) and 'The Marble Arches, Coliseum, Rome (c.1925, untraced). When Preston Art Gallery was considering the purchase of the 'Baths of Caracalla' from the London dealer Colnaghi, to whom it had been sold by Cameron, he told the gallery that 'my friends tell me it is my best architectural work and I always like such to be in public galleries'[17]

Throughout the busy 1920s Cameron escaped when he could to the

PLATE 72
Balquhidder *1931*
Drypoint, 8⅞ × 13
Private Collection

Scottish Highlands, where he found peace and solitude. He continued his series of Scottish landscapes. 'The Shadows of Glencoe' (1925, pl.75), exhibited at the RA in 1925, is a notable example. However, such interludes tended to be brief. In 1925 Cameron accepted an invitation from J. H. Whitley, the Speaker of the House of Commons from 1921 to 1928, to act as 'Master Painter' for a project to decorate eight panels in St. Stephen's Hall, which connects one of the entrances to the Houses of Parliament with the Central Lobby. St. Stephen's Hall had served as the Chamber of the House of Commons until its destruction by fire in 1834. It had been rebuilt around 1850 to a design by Sir Charles Barry as a reconstruction of the Gothic chapel which had stood on the site since 1348. In the 1920s it was decided to fill the wall panels with eight historical paintings, depicting the history of Britain from Alfred the Great to the Union of the Parliaments in 1707 under the general title 'The Building of Britain'. The theme for each painting had been chosen by Sir Henry Newbolt. Cameron was given the difficult tasks of choosing the eight artists and acting as adviser and director. It was important to preserve the individuality and freedom of each artist,

PLATE 73
Pietros, Rome c.1924
Oil on canvas, 14¾ x 12
Private Collection

but it was equally important to ensure unity and harmony, both with the structure of the interior, which is dominated by tall stained glass windows above each panel and a mosaic pavement in a geometric pattern below, and with each individual painting.

Cameron found all of the artists but one (Vivian Forbes) from within the Faculty of Painting at the British School at Rome. The artists and themes are: Colin Gill *King Alfred*; Glyn Philpott *Richard I*; Charles Sims *King John at Runnymede*; George Clausen *Wycliffe*; Vivian Forbes *Sir Thomas More*; A. K. Lawrence *Queen Elizabeth and Raleigh*; William Rothenstein *Foundation of British Influence in India*; Thomas Monnington *Union of Parliaments*.

It was anticipated that the project would take three years to complete, but it was unveiled by the Prime Minister Stanley Baldwin on 29th June 1927. Baldwin announced that in honour of the occasion George V had conferred a knighthood on George Clausen as representing the artists.

In a review of the paintings in its issue on 28th June *The Times* declared the scheme 'a great success', continuing:

'It is clear that the direction and control of Sir D. Y. Cameron, RA, has been as elastic as it has been firm in essentials, and that the artists have been as intelligent as loyal in collaboration'.

The Speaker wrote to Cameron to thank him:

'... It was indeed a lucky day when Lord Crawford answered my query by saying 'Cameron is the man, if you can get him.' Without you I do not think we could have carried the thing through to success; your ready understanding of the spirit of the place was the great asset; then there was your sure choice of the men who could see and feel that cooperation involved no derogation from individuality; and, above all, there was your happy personality making your leadership a joy to all'.[18]

The artists too expressed their thanks to Cameron, making a gift to him of the studies for the paintings in 'appreciation of the courage which prompted you to make yourself responsible for a most difficult undertaking' and adding 'that you carried us with you throughout the work is eloquent testimony to your impartiality and understanding'.[19]

The unveiling of the panels had a somewhat bizarre sequel. Tom Johnston, the Labour member for Dundee, asked in the House of Commons why the only scene depicting an incident from Scottish history dealt with an 'act of national humiliation' – the abrogation of power in favour of the Westminster Parliament – and whether any other subject had been considered. He suggested that a tablet should be fixed underneath the panel detailing the names of the Scottish Commissioners and the amounts of the bribes which they had accepted to vote in favour of the Union.[20] Exactly a week later Johnston put down a motion in the House, supported by twenty-four other Scottish members, suggesting that the salary of Lord Peel, who as First Commissioner of Works was responsible for the Houses of Parliament, should be reduced in protest at the inclusion of the painting.[21]

The Camerons returned to the south of France in March 1926, staying at the Winter Palace in Nice. They worked their way eastwards along the

PLATE 74
Baths of Caracalla, Rome *1924*
Oil on canvas, 41½ × 35½
Harris Art Gallery, Preston

coast, visiting Villefranche twice, Cap Ferrat and Monte Carlo, where they went to the Casino 'visiting the abominable gaming tables and watching the depraved types at them & on the Promenade'.[22] They also made a number of excursions from Nice to the ancient villages of Eze, perched on a rock crowned by the ruins of a 13th century castle, La Turbi, Falicon and St. Paul-de-Vence. It seems possible that the wonderful oil 'En Provence' (pl.76) dates from this visit, rather than that of 1922, as the painting first appeared at David Croal Thomson's Barbizon House gallery in London in 1927 titled 'Ruelle Obscure, Provence' – a dark alley in Provence – and was illustrated in *Thirty Years of British Art* by Sir Joseph Duveen, published in 1930.

A fellow Scot, Thomson was a close friend of Cameron and one of a small number of trusted dealers through whom at one time or another Cameron sold work. Early in his career Cameron sold etchings through the Glasgow firm of T. & R. Annan & Sons; James Craig Annan and he were great friends. In 1899 he signed an agreement with James Connell & Sons in Glasgow, appointing the firm as his agent. However, the relationship got off to a bad start. In 1900 Cameron's 'London Set' of etchings was published by the London print dealer Richard Gutekunst. Connells were furious and somewhat acrimonious correspondence passed between Connells, their lawyer and Cameron.[23] The argument was settled when it was agreed that the 'London Set' could be sold in Scotland only through Connells. A further dispute arose in 1902, but thereafter there seem to have been no further problems and Connells sold Cameron's paintings as well as etchings in both their Glasgow and London galleries until the early 1930s. Despite the shaky start Cameron and James Connell became good friends. David Croal Thomson established his own gallery in 1918 and called it Barbizon House after

PLATE 75
Shadows of Glencoe *1925*
Oil on canvas, 36 × 42
Perth Museum & Art Gallery

his major work *The Barbizon School of Painters*, which was published in 1890. Thomson dealt in Cameron's oil paintings until his death in 1930. Cameron's 'Berwick Bridge' (*c.*1906, Flemings) was in Thomson's personal collection. The Glasgow dealer Ian MacNicol acted as Cameron's agent from the early 1930s until Cameron's death in 1945. The two men became close friends. MacNicol was to continue to champion Cameron's work until his own death in 1979.

In January 1928 the Camerons were back in Rome again, visiting the British School for the third time. Cameron spent many hours with the students, which confirmed his view of the great value of the School. He wrote to Sir Evelyn Shaw 'There are some fine fellows there with real purpose and surely with a future before them'.[24] After a period in Rome the Camerons went south to Naples, before returning home. 'Ostia' (Aberdeen) and 'The Roman Campagna' (Kelvingrove, Glasgow), exhibited at the RSA in 1930 and 1938 respectively, both date from this visit.

The same year that the panels in St. Stephen's Hall were unveiled, Cameron was asked to undertake a similar role by the Bank of England. Sir John Soane's single-storey building was being demolished, except for his classical outer walls, and the present building erected under the direction of

PLATE 76
En Provence c.1926
Oil on canvas, 26¼ × 32½
National Gallery of Scotland

the architect Sir Herbert Baker. The Bank had decided to commission a number of paintings in order to provide a measure of decoration for the largely plain interior walls. The theme was to be 'The Bank in Being', a contemporary account of the personnel and work of the Bank. The paintings would comprise single portraits and group activities, all against backgrounds depicting the building which was being demolished. Cameron was to advise on the choice of artists and to supervise their work.

The artists finally chosen were: Sir George Clausen; Francis Dodd; Colin Gill; A. K. Lawrence; Thomas Monnington; Sir William Rothenstein; W. W. Russell. Again, all the painters, with the exception of Dodd, were connected with the British School at Rome.

The task facing Cameron was a daunting one. The project was larger than the St. Stephen's Hall scheme, involving around fourteen paintings of varying sizes and shapes. On the one hand he had to liaise with Sir Herbert Baker and certain of the Bank's senior management and on the other he had to act as friend, counsellor and occasional slave-driver to the artists. Inevitably, there were worrying delays in the completion of some of the paintings; Lawrence had almost fifty portraits to do and he fell well behind schedule. Several paintings required some measure of reworking when they were seen *in situ* in order for them to harmonise better with their surroundings or with adjacent works.

A number of the paintings were exhibited at the RA in 1932. Reviewing them for *The Times*, Frank Rutter thought that they were very unexciting:

> 'Most of us agree that in colour and design these paintings are inoffensive to the eye; but the trouble is, alas! that they neither excite emotion nor inspire the mind'.[25]

However, Rutter conceded that the fault lay in the choice of subject matter, rather than with the artists.

Cameron acknowledged that St. Stephen's Hall was a simple matter compared with this project.[26] Even when the rebuilding itself was finished in 1938 and the paintings could be hung in their chosen locations, some work remained to be done. In July of that year Sir Herbert Baker wrote to Cameron:

PLATE 77
Ben Lomond c.*1922*
Watercolour over charcoal, 7 x 13¼
Flemings

'This work has indeed extended beyond any anticipation in the matter of time and I am afraid, apart from time, your job has involved more difficulties and worries than were anticipated. I am inclined to think that in many respects we are better pleased than you are and that is quite as it should be, for you have a standard in these matters that is more like a dream than a realisable fact'.[27]

In a letter to Mr. A. V. Alexander, the Secretary of the Bank of England, Sir Herbert Baker confided that:

'Cameron is a man who devotes much more time to public work than is good for his health or his art'.[28]

It was a concern which was shared by several relatives and friends. His brother James had tried to raise the issue with him:

'He became very sullen and impatient when I ventured to tell him from various sources how his public life here and there was affecting his art. He was deeply wounded, he said. He has never learnt the art of speech (for I tried to deal with that also) but I fear that displeased him'.[29]

His brother thought that 'his head has perhaps been turned by success'.[30] However, Cameron had a strong sense of duty. He felt that it was not enough to paint. An artist had a wider responsibility to foster art in general and assist its institutions when he could.

[1] T. P. Wiseman, *A Short History of the British School at Rome*, London, 1990, p.17

[2] Ibid., p.15

[3] Minutes of meeting of Faculty of Painting, 14th February 1923 (Archives of British School at Rome, London)

[4] Minutes of meeting of Faculty of Painting, 10th January 1924 (Archives of British School at Rome, London)

[5] Note prepared by Sir Evelyn Shaw for Rev. Sam Compton (Cameron's brother-in-law and compiler of Cameron's entry in *Dictionary of National Biography*)

[6] Letter from Private Secretary to Lloyd George to Cameron dated 19th May 1920 (NLS ACC8950.4)

[7] Letter from Cameron to James Connell dated 3rd July 1921 (NLS ACC7797.4)

[8] Undated press cutting (NLS ACC8950.41)

[9] Obituary, *The Times*, 18th September 1945

[10] Sir James Caw, 'Sir D. Y. Cameron', *Old Watercolour Society Club* Vol.27, 1949 p.9

[11] RSA Annual Report 1945

[12] Letter from Lady Cameron to Evelyn Shaw dated 2nd September 1921 (Archives of British School at Rome, London)

[13] Letter from Cameron to Sydney Cockerell dated 19th January 1922 (Fitzwilliam Museum, Cambridge)

[14] Letter from Charles Aitken to Cameron dated 16th March 1922 (NLS ACC8950.1)

[15] Letter from Cameron to James Connell dated 26th November 1920 (NLS ACC7797.4)

[16] Letter from Cameron to James Connell dated 17th February 1923 (NLS ACC7797.4)

[17] Letter from Cameron to Mr. Hamilton dated 16th May 1924 (Preston Art Gallery)

[18] Letter from J. H. Whiteley to Cameron dated 30th June 1927 (NLS ACC8950.1)

[19] Letter to Cameron signed by all the artists except Charles Sims, who was in America at the time

[20] *The Times*, 1st July 1927

[21] *The Times*, 8th July 1927

[22] Letter from Cameron to Sir George Henschel dated 15th March 1926 (NLS ACC6211.13)

[23] See letters from Cameron to Connells NLS ACC7797.1

[24] Letter from Cameron to Sir Evelyn Shaw dated 11th January 1928 (Archives of British Scool at Rome, London)

[25] *The Times*, 1st May 1932

[26] Letter from Cameron to Sir Herbert Baker dated 4th January 1936 (Archives of Bank of England Museum)

[27] Letter from Sir Herbert Baker to Cameron dated 28th July 1938 (Archives of Bank of England Museum)

[28] Letter from Sir Herbert Baker to A. V. Alexander dated 16th April 1930 (Archives of Bank of England Museum)

[29] Letter from James Cameron to his sister Katharine dated 31st May 1929 (Watt)

[30] Letter from James Cameron to Katharine dated 7th July 1929 (Watt)

CHAPTER NINE

'THE TIME OF DARKNESS'

SIR FRANK DICKSEE, THE PRESIDENT OF THE RA, DIED IN
October 1928. Cameron was urged to stand for the Presidency, but he
declined to be nominated. It was a measure of his high standing with his
fellow artists – in England as well as Scotland – that he would have stood an
excellent chance of being elected as the RA's thirteenth President. Certainly
the London correspondent of the *Glasgow Herald* thought so:

> 'There is, I believe, no question that Sir D. Y. Cameron would have received
> overwhelming support had it not been for the determination he reached after
> careful consideration of the position alike from the public and personal
> standpoints'.[1]

This view is confirmed by a letter to Cameron from Sir Charles Holmes, the
landscape painter and critic, who was Director of the National Gallery from
1916 to 1928:

> 'May I send a line to say with what heartfelt regret I heard the news that you
> couldn't stand for the Presidency. You were the hope of all who wished to see
> unity and harmony restored to our national artistic efforts and carried a weight
> in virtue of your own great achievements that no other man however
> fairminded and public spirited could bring to the task of reconstruction'.[2]

Holmes was referring to disagreements between the RA and the Trustees of
the Tate Gallery over the Chantrey Bequest, which had broken out again in
1927 and 1928 and soured the relationship between the two bodies. The RA
had refused to purchase recommended works from the New English Art
Club's exhibition and the Tate had stayed away from the usual meeting to
consider purchases from the RA's Summer Exhibition.[3]

The correspondent of the *Glasgow Herald* had ascribed Cameron's reasons
for declining nomination to the necessity of residing in London for the
greater part of the year and to the effect that the various duties and
responsibilities would have on his art. Certainly these must have featured in
Cameron's reasoning. However, a more important point was his anxiety
over the health of his wife. Lady Cameron had been in hospital that year and
had returned home shortly before a decision had to be taken about whether
to stand or not. It is almost certain that she had been treated for cancer. It
seems probable that in the circumstances Cameron did not want to burden
his wife with Presidential duties or be away from home for long periods.

The re-union of the Church of Scotland and the United Free Church
took place on 2nd October 1929. The Assemblies of the two Churches met
that afternoon in Edinburgh in the Industrial Hall in Annandale Street.
Cameron had been responsible for designing 'a scheme of daring, but
harmonious decoration'[4], which had transformed the vast gloomy Hall into

PLATE 78
The Moors of Mearns c.1936
Pen & brown wash, 6¼ × 9½
Private Collection

a 'place of singular beauty and seemliness' for the massed congregation of some 12,000 people.[5] It must have gladdened Cameron's heart that the United Free Church, formed in 1900 by the union of the Free Church and the United Presbyterian Church – his father's church and the one into which he himself had been baptised – had come back to the fold. Cameron was a staunch supporter of the established order, whether in art or in the church. Indeed, when the Camerons resided in London, they worshipped not with the Church of Scotland but with the Church of England (and 'High Church' at that).[6]

The same year the Cotswold Gallery in London held an exhibition of Cameron's watercolours of the Scottish Highlands, together with several examples of scenes in Cairo and Venice. Cameron is seen at his best in his watercolours, particularly those which are little more than sketches. Yet he was surprised that these were so popular, writing to Martin Hardie, the watercolourist and Keeper of Prints and Drawings at the Victoria & Albert Museum from 1921 to 1935:

'I am never done wondering why collectors wish my simple things, just impressions of beautiful days and places, often in preparation for, or a change from, heavier oil work or the exacting copper plate and its unpleasant technicalities'. [7]

Cameron did not seem to appreciate that they are liked because they are so fresh, so spontaneous. They are rarely mannered or laboured, criticisms which can be levelled at some of his oils. His fine draughtsmanship, elegant design and subtle use of colour is exemplified in 'Kinloch Aline' (Flemings), which was included in the Cotswold exhibition, 'Loch Lomond' (pl.80) and 'In Ross' (pl.79). D. S. Meldrum, writing in *Apollo*, summed it up well:

PLATE 79
In Ross c.1934
Watercolour, 5¾ × 6⅝
Private Collection

'Two qualities at least may be safely ascribed to these drawings of the Highlands: the spirit of place, and a sense of style, that blend it is which gives them their peculiar great distinction'[8]

The Camerons were ardent supporters of their church in Kippen. It had been renovated completely in the mid-1920s, due in no small measure to the faith and enterprise of its minister, the Rev. John Younie, and the advice and resources of Cameron. He and his wife had gifted the oak ceiling with its series of crosses, each with a special significance. Cameron was passionate in his desire to see beauty reintroduced into Scottish churches; he lectured on the subject on many occasions. He was also a firm believer in the need for symbolism in worship. The hand of Cameron can be seen everywhere in the church – the style of decoration, the degree of ornamentation, the design of the panels of embroidery worked by the ladies of the congregation, the symbolism of the objects placed throughout the church, many gifted by members of the congregation or the Camerons themselves over the years. The taste and craftsmanship are of a very high order. Cameron placed great stress on craftsmanship. He campaigned for a revival in craft skills, believing that they merited a much greater emphasis in the education system than they were accorded. Kippen Parish Church truly enshrines Cameron's twin principles of beauty and symbolism. However, the style of renovation was not to everyone's liking; there was an under-current of concern that the spirit of Presbyterianism was being compromised in the manner and degree of ornamentation. Indeed it seems strange that Cameron – the son of a Presbyterian minister, an artist of austere landscapes – should embrace a style of church decoration and symbolism so closely identified with the 'Auld Religion'. Yet he was strongly in favour of an Episcopalian manner of decoration; a number of years later he wrote to his sister:

'You know, Katie, that there is nothing for you in Presbyterianism – you must have the art and order of Episcopacy. I feel this more and more every Sunday.

PLATE 80
Loch Lomond c.1926
Watercolour, 5¾ x 8¼
Private Collection

Presbyterianism leaves me hungry and dissatisfied. It is not worship in the true sense, it is just listening.'[9]

On the other hand he staunchly defended the Church of Scotland's traditional austere and simple dignity of worship.[10]

In July 1931 the Church House was dedicated. The Camerons had purchased the land adjoining Kippen Parish Church for £900 and had met the cost of constructing the building, which was to be used as a Session House and Guild Room.[11] In addition, they gifted almost all the contents, including a bronze 'Entry into Jerusalem' by Alfred Hardiman, which Cameron had specially commissioned for the church.[12]

Less than four months later Lady Cameron died at the age of 60. After apparently conquering cancer in 1928, she had become ill again some two years later. 'The summer and autumn have been one long sorrow and anxiety' Cameron later wrote to his nephew Robert Cameron Watt.[13] When death did come, he was devastated. It was a blow from which he never really recovered. They had known each other for 42 years and had been married for 35; '... the many years together were a long romance, gathering beauty from 1889 when I first met her – even unto the very end'.[14]

She was a great companion – they did everything together – and she had encouraged and supported him in his work. A charming person, she was universally loved. She was very fond of children, whereas Cameron always felt awkward with them, probably because he was not used to them, having none of their own. Thoughtful and kind-hearted, she was a lady in the true sense of the word, equally at home in the village or in Academy circles. After her death their close friend Frank Rinder wrote:

'In countless hearts and homes her innate sympathy and inspiring presence quickened beauty of mind, heart and spirit.[15]

Lady Cameron also was very artistic. A skilled embroiderer, she encouraged the ladies of Kippen Parish Church to take up embroidery. Cameron himself drew the designs for the women to execute. The finished work was sold to raise funds for the church. Some of the items are exquisite and there was much demand for them. In Perth Museum and Art Gallery there is an antique mahogany pole screen with a striking peacock panel embroidered by Lady Cameron, which came from Dun Eaglais.

After her death Cameron's life could never be the same again. For a long time he was overwhelmed by the loss, later describing the period to Sir James Caw as 'the time of darkness'.[16] In 1932 he wrote to Sir George Henschel:

'Life is not now as it was – & I find dimness & darkness surrounding me everywhere & disinclination for so many things which just recall Jean & make me sorrowful.[17]

He gave up the London house and returned permanently to Scotland. In 1932 he was reinstated as a full member of the RSA. The following year Sir George Washington Browne, the RSA's tenth President, retired at the age of 80. Cameron, then aged 68, was approached for a second time about standing for the Presidency. However, he declined:

'After thirty years of constant public work in various directions I felt I had to decline. I could not accept without retiring from many things & that I felt unable to do at once – hence my decision. But it would have been a great pleasure to have succeeded our wonderful Sir James Guthrie & to have had the pleasure of working with you. But, dreams vanish & life wanes'.[18]

The same day that he declined to be nominated, he wrote to the RSA, asking to be transferred to the list of Honorary Retired Members 'in order to hasten promotion from Associate rank to full membership' – promotion to Academician depended entirely on the death or retiral of an existing Academician. He added that he had 'many regrets in asking this, but in the best interests of the Academy it is well there should be swifter promotion & I hope other senior members will make the same request'.[19]

The intense depression which enveloped Cameron lifted only very slowly. His many friends were a great support to him at this time. Sadly Sir

PLATE 82

Castle Urquhart, Loch Ness c.1930

Oil on canvas, 11½ × 29½

Private Collection

James Guthrie had died in 1930, but Frank Rinder, Sir James Caw, together with their wives, and Sir George Henschel and his daughter Helen were frequent visitors to Dun Eaglais. Cameron had known Henschel, the singer, composer and first conductor of the Scottish Orchestra, for many years and had stayed with him at Alltnacriche, the house which Henschel had built near Alvie not far from Aviemore. When Henschel died in 1935, Helen, who was a very fine singer herself, continued to visit Dun Eaglais and sang on several occasions in Kippen Parish Church. For Cameron music was a great comfort and inspiration throughout his life; indeed, he loved music second only to art. In happier times his 'clan' would gather together at Dun Eaglais every New Year's Day to listen to Handel's 'Messiah'.[20]

Cameron's continued involvement with Kippen Parish Church was also a source of comfort. He had been made an elder of the church on Christmas Sunday 1928 and frequently represented the church at the annual General Assembly of the Church of Scotland in Edinburgh. Later he was one of the original sponsors of the Iona Community. He was very friendly with Dr. George Macleod, the Community's founder, and attended most of the meetings of the sponsors in Edinburgh.

Over the thirteen years or so until his death in 1945 he devoted himself to his painting, to advising the many Scottish churches which sought his help with their programmes of rebuilding and redecoration and to his other public duties and responsibilities. He continued as a member of the Board of Trustees of the National Galleries of Scotland until his death. In 1933 he was made a member of the Royal Fine Art Commission for Scotland, taking the place of the sculptor James Pittendrigh Macgillivray. The following year he was appointed Vice-convenor of the Church of Scotland's Advisory Committee on Artistic Questions.

What was to be his last print was the drypoint 'The Broken Crucifix' (R.500), which he executed in 1932.[21] He gave up etching shortly after his wife's death, although later he talked about taking up the needle again:

> 'As to plates, I have felt so 'off' etching for the last years that it is difficult to turn to it. However, it is ever in my mind & I really have one or two in the copper if I could bring myself to complete them.'[22]

Sadly, he never did. To many 'The Broken Crucifix' seemed a poignant reminder of Lady Cameron's own suffering. Cameron told his sister Katharine that 'It was drawn from an ancient and crumbling fragment during our last journey to Oberammergau and is full of memories'.[23]

The Camerons had been very keen on mystery plays. For several years before her death Lady Cameron had devised and directed a number of nativity and mystery plays at Kippen Parish Church. The last one was performed only the previous Christmas Eve, an occasion both of joy and sorrow, for on the Christmas morning Cameron's sister Marie, who though very ill had enjoyed the previous evening's performance in the church, died. A widow for over thirty years, she held a special place in Cameron's affections.

Cameron produced in 1932 a large series of sepia drawings to illustrate Seton Gordon's books *Highways and Byways in the West Highlands* and

Highways and Byways in the Central Highlands published in 1935 and 1948 respectively. They demonstrate Cameron's wonderful draughtsmanship and sense of design. 'Tay at Stanley' (pl.83) is an example. He had known Seton Gordon, the nature photographer and writer, for many years, both sharing a love for the remote places of Scotland. Over the years Cameron had provided illustrations for a number of books. Between 1889 and 1901 he had etched twenty-three plates for the Regality Club, which had been established in Glasgow in 1885 to preserve a record of the city's old buildings, many of which were demolished subsequently. The first book which Cameron illustrated was the Border Edition of Sir Walter Scott's *Waverley* novels, published in London in 1892-94, for which he supplied nine etchings. This was followed by etchings for reproduction in a number of other books, including twenty plates for the Winchester Edition of *The Compleat Angler* by Isaak Walton, which was published in London in 1902. In general, Cameron's illustrations are disappointing, due partly to the paper used and the mass printing process, but also because in many instances his inspiration seemed to fail him when executing commissions. Exceptions are the wash drawings he did for Sir Herbert Maxwell's *The Story of the Tweed*. This lavish volume was published by James Nisbet of London in 1905 at the very high price of five guineas – an indication of the care which went into its production. In the drawings Cameron not only captured the beauty of the Scottish Borders, but also its romantic spirit and its fiery history. He was not to undertake any further illustrations for almost twenty-five years, when reproductions of ten wash drawings and an original etching were included in *The District of Menteith* by R. B. Cunninghame Graham, published by Eneas Mackay of Stirling in 1930.

From now on Cameron concentrated solely on painting the Scottish landscape in oil and watercolour. At first that vital inspiration which moved

PLATE 83
Tay at Stanley *1932*
Pen & brown wash, 7½ × 6¾
Private Collection

PLATE 84
Wilds of Assynt *1936*
Oil on canvas, 40 × 50
Perth Museum & Art Gallery

him to paint was lacking. As late as September 1933 he wrote:

> 'I have little to show and destroy most I do, and never wish to exhibit any
> more; they only make me unhappy and destroy all the best qualities one aims
> at'.[24]

He regained his spirit gradually, though he was to suffer recurring bouts of
loneliness and depression for the rest of his life. He found solace in
Scotland's hills and rivers, her mountains and lochs, the beauty of which, he
said in a letter to one of his friends, he 'felt sometimes overwhelming'[25].
His paintings of the period reflect this. Sometimes he appears guilty of
exaggeration, both in terms of colour and grandiose design, until, that is,
one comes across, usually in the early morning or at sunset, a scene in
reality which bears out Cameron's apparently extraordinary vision of colour
and setting – a scene which truly has to be seen to be believed. Cameron
was not concerned with the everyday scene, but with a portrayal of 'that
spell of mystic beauty, haunted by strangeness of form and colour, remote
from the facts and feelings of common life' which he referred to in his
address on 'The Romance of Scottish History'.[26] There is almost a sense of
the Wondrous Hand of God in some of these later landscapes. Indeed, he
mentioned in a letter to his nephew Robert Cameron Watt 'I more than
ever believe in strange guidance and directions...'.[27] His palette at this time
ranged from strong pink, mauve and blue to rich browns, plum and gold.
Typical examples of this period are 'Loch Lubnaig' (c.1933, pl.86),
'Suilven' (c.1934, pl.85) and 'Wilds of Assynt' (1936, pl.84), which
Cameron regarded as his finest large oil.

Honours continued to be heaped upon him. In 1933 he was appointed
the King's Painter and Limner in Scotland on the death of Robert Gibb,
who had held the title since 1908. The office was created by Queen Anne in

PLATE 85
Suilven *1934*
Oil on canvas, 40 × 50
Michael Cox

1703, the original recipient having a commission to paint portraits of the Royal Family. However, for some time it had involved no official duties and was a means of honouring a distinguished practising artist, the title being held for the remainder of the artist's life. Raeburn and Wilkie were so honoured, although Raeburn held the title for less than two months. In 1936 St. Andrews became the fourth university to bestow on him an Honorary Degree of Doctor of Laws. Since his first degree from Glasgow in 1911, he had been similarly honoured by Manchester and Cambridge in 1923 and 1928 respectively.

At over 70 years of age Cameron was still as busy as he had ever been. He wrote to his nephew:

'My life is spent in my studio mostly and, when away, visiting and helping churches and lecturing on art'.[28]

He also had many official duties in Edinburgh in connection with the National Galleries of Scotland and the RSA. Much of his time was taken up visiting churches to advise on decoration. He travelled the length and breadth of Scotland:

'… away for 3 weeks in Fort George, Inverness & Aviemore over varied works, but now at home except for duties in Edinburgh & Glasgow almost every week. Travelling very difficult – laid up my car – no petrol'.[29]

The Very Rev. Charles Warr, the minister of St. Giles' Cathedral from 1926 to 1962, and he were closely associated in the movement to reintroduce beauty into the Scottish kirk.[30] Cameron described it as 'my chief hobby trying to make ugly churches more seemly'.[31] Many congregations had good cause to be thankful to Cameron for the guidance he gave.

PLATE 86
Loch Lubnaig c.1933
Oil on canvas, 30¼ x 35¼
Flemings

However much he was busy, there were times when he felt very lonely – 'I have found ten years of aloneness almost unbearable – without love life is a wilderness'.[32] Whatever differences there might have been in the past between his sister Katharine and him, they came together again in the 1930s. They were a great comfort to each other, particularly after Katharine's husband died in 1939. At that time Cameron had thought of moving closer to her in Edinburgh, but he must have been reluctant to leave Dun Eaglais and in the end he did not move.

In September 1945 he had a busy programme of visits:

'I am going north next week to Perth & Aviemore & then Aberdeen. I have [?]five churches to visit, the great old St. John's of Perth & St. Machar's in Aberdeen & so will meet many others seeking after better things in Church conditions in Scotland. My sisters [Katharine and Ruby] are to be with me in Perth'.[33]

On Friday 14th September he and his two sisters had attended the opening in Perth of an RSW exhibition and on the Saturday Cameron had been adding colour to the central panel of the Communion table in St. John's Church. On the Sunday evening he delivered an address entitled 'A Cry from the Heart' in St. John's Church. On his return to the Royal George Hotel, where he was staying with Katharine and Ruby, he collapsed on the front steps of the hotel. He died almost immediately from a severe heart attack.

Cameron died as he would have wished – still crusading for beauty in worship at the age of 80. For over sixty years he had zealously carried the banners for art and the Church to every corner of Scotland and beyond. Three days later he was buried beside Lady Cameron in the little cemetery a few miles outside Kippen, which looks across to his beloved Ben Ledi. Typically, his last painting, on which he had laboured long, was 'Dawn' (1945, pl.88), a view across the plain of the Forth to Ben Ledi in the distance. The following Sunday there was a Memorial Service in Kippen Parish Church; the address was given by his friend the Rev. J. Pitt Watson. Tributes to him came from many quarters. Perhaps one of the finest was from an anonymous friend who wrote to *The Times* '... and to have known him is to feel that all is not wrong with the world of men'.[34] On the same day the newspaper carried accounts of atrocities perpetrated in the Second World War.

Cameron was a true connoisseur. Over the years he and his wife had collected an amazing range of watercolours, drawings, prints, bronzes, silver, ceramics, textiles, books, furniture and rugs. As well as collections of Rembrandt's etchings and drawings by Charles Keene – the 'artists' artist', who drew for 'Punch' and whose drawings were collected by Degas – Cameron had bronzes by his friend Sir Alfred Gilbert, etchings by Alphonse Legros, pieces of Martinware – art pottery modelled by the three Martin brothers – and a large number of Persian rugs. During his lifetime Cameron gifted many items to Kippen Parish Church and to Perth Museum and Art Gallery. In 1943 he had gifted fifty-five etchings by Rembrandt to the National Galleries of Scotland. In his will Cameron directed his trustees to transfer to the National Galleries, of which he had been a member of the

PLATE 87
Isles of Morar c.1940
Oil on canvas, 26 × 36½
Private Collection

Board of Trustees for a quarter of a century, any items from his collections which they chose. The remainder was to be offered to Perth Museum, with which he had had a close association since it opened in 1935. Thus much of the Camerons' varied collections passed to public institutions.

Cameron was one of the most respected figures in the world of art in the 1920s and '30s. He was a very cultured man, a man of firm convictions and a deep religious faith, which permeated his life at all levels. Charles Warr described him as 'a fascinating personality, full of the zest of life, yet infinitely sensitive'.[35] He was that rare combination of Romantic and man of affairs. He managed to combine his painting with a full public life, not sparing himself in the service either of art and its institutions or of the Church right up to his death.

He was passionate in what he perceived as his twin roles in life – creating beauty through his painting and promoting beauty within the Church. As an artist he was renowned equally in Scotland and England, unlike most British painters who are known only in one or other of the two. He was held in high esteem by his fellow artists and by the art-conscious public alike. His work was purchased by many public galleries throughout the world, as well as by numerous private collectors, both at home and

overseas, particularly in Canada, where his vision of the romance and beauty of the Scottish landscape struck a chord.

It may be going too far to describe him as a great artist. He never depicted the human condition in any of its many states. He was not a trailblazer, but neither was he an imitator. Allied to superb draughtsmanship and technique, he had an individual conception and style, to which he remained true throughout his life. Many of his oils are wonderful in their power and drama, but it is in his etchings and his watercolours that his true worth can be seen.

Cameron will be remembered as one of the leading Scottish landscape painters. His is a powerful evocation of the beauty and grandeur of the Scottish landscape. In a radio broadcast to mark the centenary of his birth the artist Sir William MacTaggart said 'He was one of the few artists who succeeded in capturing the drama of the Highlands'.[36] However, he deserves to be remembered also for his architectural subjects. Few artists can compare with Cameron in his portrayal of the character and spirit of a building, whether it be a magnificent cathedral or a medieval house.

A Memorial Exhibition was organised by the Scottish Committee of the Arts Council in 1947, which was shown in Glasgow, Aberdeen, Dundee, Paisley and Perth. In 1965 the Arts Council mounted a comprehensive exhibition of his work at Kelvingrove Art Gallery in Glasgow to celebrate the centenary of his birth. Part of the exhibition toured to a number of centres within Scotland. Until now Alasdair Auld's catalogue for the Centenary Exhibition stood as the only substantial post-War tribute to Cameron.

The intervening years have been unkind to Cameron. Today he is largely forgotten outside Scotland. He is considered to be rather 'old fashioned', regarded as being concerned with subject-matter rather than the sensuous qualities of paint, which so exercise artists today. But the tide will turn and the intrinsic integrity of Cameron's art will be rediscovered.

1   *Glasgow Herald*, 11th December 1928
2   Letter from C. J. Holmes to Cameron dated 8th November 1928 (NLS ACC8950.1)
3   Sidney C. Hutchison, *History of the Royal Academy*, 2nd edition, London, 1986, p.152
4   Charles L. Warr, *The Glimmering Landscape*, London, 1960, p.300
5   R. W. A. Begg, *The Renovation of Kippen Parish Church*, 5th edition, 1986, p.9
6   Watt

7   Martin Hardie, *Water-Colour Painting in Britain*, Vol.III, London, 1968, p.211
8   D. S. Meldrum, 'Sir David Cameron's Watercolours of the Highlands', *Apollo*, October 1929, pp.220-2
9   Letter from Cameron to his sister Katharine dated between 1939 and 1944 (Watt)
10 Charles L. Warr, op. cit., p.216
11 Strictly the church was known as Christ Church from 1929 and did not become Kippen Parish Church until its amalgamation with Muirhead Church in 1944
12 Begg, op. cit., p.31
13 Watt
14 Ibid.
15 Rinder, p.xxvii
16 Sir James Caw, 'Sir D. Y. Cameron', *Old Watercolour Society Club*, Vol.27, 1949 p.4
17 Letter from Cameron to Sir George Henschel dated 26th July 1932 (NLS ACC6211.13)
18 Letter from Cameron to Assistant Secretary of RSA dated 4th November 1933 (Archives of RSA)
19 Letter from Cameron to Secretary of RSA dated 4th November 1933 (Archives of RSA)
20 Watt
21 His last etching may have been a book plate for Andrew Reid, which was executed in 1932 but omitted by Rinder
22 Letter from Cameron to H. J. L. Wright dated 20th May 1935 (NLS ACC3255)
23 Letter from Cameron to his sister Katharine (unknown date) (Watt)
24 Letter from Cameron to his sister Katharine dated September 1933 (Watt)
25 H. J. L. Wright, *Etchings & Drypoints of Sir D. Y. Cameron*, The Print Collectors' Club, No. 24, 1947, p.26
26 See Chapter Seven
27 Letter from Cameron to Robert Cameron Watt dated 30th May 1938 (Watt)
28 Letter from Cameron to Robert Cameron Watt dated 26th April 1945 (Watt)
29 Letter from Cameron to Robert Cameron Watt dated 12th June 1942 (Watt)
30 Charles L. Warr, op. cit.
31 Letter from Cameron to Robert Cameron Watt dated 15th October 1941 (Watt)
32 Letter from Cameron to his sister Katharine between 1939 & 1944 (Watt)
33 Letter from Cameron to Robert Cameron Watt dated 7th September 1945 (Watt)
34 *The Times*, 22nd September 1945
35 Charles L. Warr, op.cit., p.216
36 Sir William MacTaggart speaking on 'Scottish Life and Letters', BBC Scottish Home Service, ? June 1965 (NLS ACC8950)

CHAPTER TEN

'WHERE THE BEE SUCKS'

ON HER RETURN FROM HER STUDIES AT COLAROSSI'S IN Paris in 1902, Katharine Cameron was asked by the publishers T. C. and E. C. Jack to illustrate a book for children. It was to be called *In Fairyland* and would contain a number of familiar fairy tales edited by Louey Chisholm. Even if Jack's art editor had not seen her exhibition at the Glasgow galleries of James Connell & Sons in 1900, H. C. Marillier's article in *The Art Journal* the following year, praising her skilful drawing and composition and the rich colour of her fairies and goblins, must have drawn her to the publishers' attention.

Katharine was delighted to be paid for doing something she loved. She eagerly set to work, rereading the stories and using as models her relatives and friends, including her brother D.Y. and Anna Buchan. Published in 1904 at a price of seven shillings and sixpence, *In Fairyland* contained thirty illustrations by her. She also executed the cover design and end papers. Over the following decade or so she was to produce many more illustrations for the same publishers.

In 1904 Katharine was 30 years old, an attractive and vivacious young

PLATE 89
Snowdrops and Bee *1914*
Watercolour, 7 x 7⅛
Private Collection

woman. Already she had gained a reputation as a watercolourist of considerable talent. At the early age of 22 she had been elected to the RSW. Since 1900 she had lived with her widowed mother and her older sisters Joanna and Marie, along with Marie's young son Robert, in a large house in Victoria Square in Stirling, in which she had her studio. Marie, who sadly had been widowed at the age of 33, kept house and looked after them all. D. Y. Cameron contributed to the upkeep of both house and household.

When he was about five years old, Robert acted as the model for Katharine's next book – an edition by Jack of Charles Kingsley's classic for children *The Water-Babies*. She provided eight illustrations for the book, which was published in 1905. Other children's books followed in rapid succession, including *Stories of King Arthur's Knights* by Mary Macgregor (1905), *The Enchanted Land* by Louey Chisholm (1906), for which she produced thirty illustrations and the binding design, *The Story of Undine* (published by Thos. Nelson in 1907), *Aucassin & Nicolette* (published by T. N. Foulis in 1908), *Legends & Stories of Italy for Children* by Amy Steedman (1909), *Celtic Tales* by Louey Chisholm (1910) and *Rhymes of the Duchess May* (published by Foulis around 1912). Her first book *In Fairyland* was reissued in 1910 in six separate parts, to which she contributed an additional eighteen plates.

Katharine's illustrations are varied and colourful. However, she did not develop a distinctive style, unlike her contemporary Jessie King, and there is little to distinguish them from the illustrations in the multitude of children's books which were produced in the early days of colour printing. Her work is competent, but, with a few exceptions, somewhat unexciting. The exceptions include several plates in *Legends and Stories of Italy*, particularly the very different 'Madonna' and 'Beatrice and Marziale', the former being in a fine decorative style – her mother was the model for the Madonna. When her illustrations are compared with her other work of the period, one is left with a feeling of disappointment, which is not entirely due to the comparatively poor quality of colour printing at the time. Part of the answer lies in her apparent lack of real commitment to illustration. What she really wanted to do was to paint flowers. Her attitude towards her work as an illustrator was summed up well in a conversation which she had with John Russell Taylor in 1960. In his book *The Art Nouveau Book in Britain* Taylor recounts that:

> 'she drifted into book-illustration … because she was asked to, went on illustrating as long as people went on asking her, and then returned happily to landscape and flower-painting with never a second thought, only keeping some of her books, which she never took seriously, on the insistence of her husband'.[1]

The difference in quality between her illustrative work and her true watercolours can be appreciated when one looks at the books in which her flower studies are reproduced, particularly *Flowers I Love*, an anthology of poems chosen by Philip E. Thomas and published by Jack in 1916, and *Where the Bee Sucks*, another collection of poems chosen by Iolo A. Williams and published by The Medici Society in 1929. The plates for the latter books

PLATE 90
Allongia
Watercolour
Private Collection

were not done specifically as illustrations; they are photographs of existing watercolours in a variety of styles, which she had executed over a period. The watercolours 'Allongia' (pl.90) and 'Black eyed Daisies' (back jacket) are reproduced in *Flowers I Love*.

In addition to the work for her publishers, Katharine continued to paint watercolours of flowers – still lifes and studies of flowers – as well as figure subjects and several portraits. About 1900 she had begun to execute landscapes. She was now sending work regularly to the annual exhibitions of the RSA and the Society of Scottish Artists, as well as the RGI and the RSW. She was elected a Member of the SSA in 1909.

In 1908 Mrs. Cameron and her daughters, together with Marie's son Robert, who by then was ten years old, moved from Stirling to Edinburgh. The move may have been aimed at assisting Katharine's career as an artist – Edinburgh was still the art centre of Scotland, although its relative importance was diminishing. A year later they were joined by Ruby, who had acted as housekeeper for her brother James until his marriage that year. The Camerons lived at 10 George Square for three or four years, before moving to 53 George Square. Katharine had a studio at 4 Forres Street. In 1911 or early 1912 she took a flat at 108 George Street, which she held until her marriage in 1928.

Katharine resumed her etching in earnest in 1911. She had etched her first plate, 'Wild Bees', in 1898, but it was not until 1909 that she executed two further plates, 'April' and 'The Tryst'. Her first set of eight etchings of flowers was printed and published by T. & R. Annan & Sons of Glasgow in 1911. Over the next 25 years or so she etched another 73 plates at least, making a total of 84 or more.[2] Just over two-thirds are etchings of flowers and/or insects. The remainder, almost all executed in etching and drypoint, consist of landscapes – mainly of Scotland, but also several scenes in the south of England – and a few architectural subjects, including an inn in Normandy. Most of her etchings are characterised by a strong but delicate line. Virtually all her flower studies are populated by bees or butterflies, which, though charming in a single impression, become somewhat tedious when viewed as a group. She gave several of her etchings humorous titles – two caterpillars on a flower stalk is titled 'The Race' and a snail moving along a twig 'Flitting', the Scots word for moving house.

Katharine exhibited for the first time at the RA in London in 1912, showing an etching 'Thistledown'. However, she did not submit any further work – etchings or watercolours – until 1921; thereafter, she exhibited on an irregular basis until 1963. She showed four of her etchings at the RE in 1920, when she was elected an Associate of that Society; Hester Frood, her fellow student at Colarossi's in Paris, was elected at the same time. Right up to her death in 1965 she was a regular exhibitor at the RE, failing to submit work on only four occasions over the next 45 years, even though to all intents and purposes she gave up etching in 1938. She was elected a Fellow of the RE in 1964.

In 1918 or early the next year Katharine's mother and sisters Joanna and Marie moved to 30 Regent Terrace in Edinburgh. Ruby had left home in 1913, following her marriage to the Rev. Sam Compton, a Presbyterian

PLATE 91
Goatsbeard *1915*
Etching, $14\frac{3}{4} \times 5\frac{1}{4}$
Private Collection

minister from Ulster. She was very pretty and had had a number of suitors, but Mrs. Cameron was rather possessive and wanted to keep her daughters around her for as long as possible. Only Minnie had managed to fly the nest at the relatively young age of 23. Marie was 31 when she married, Ruby was 35 and Katharine was 54. Joanna was never to marry; she spent a lifetime working for social and charitable causes, dying from cancer in 1920 two days before her fifty-seventh birthday.

Katharine was concentrating now on flower studies and landscapes. She later told Tom Honeyman 'there is nothing so inspiring as painting flowers'.[3] Like her brother, she had dedicated herself to expressing in her watercolours the beauty and diversity of nature, whether it be the landscape or its flowers and plants. She held the view that:

> 'Art, in a sense, is a Gospel — good news, which is intended to bring delight, reverence for all living things and joy in the natural phenomenon of mountains, lochs and seas'.[4]

Her draughtsmanship and use of colour are excellent. She believed that drawing lay at the very heart of painting, taking issue with those moderns who considered that drawing was unimportant. In later life she disliked most art after 1920, describing the artists as 'ill' if in her estimation they did not draw properly.[5]

Katharine married Arthur Kay on 17th April 1928 in the Moray Aisle of St Giles' Cathedral in Edinburgh; Ruby's husband Sam Compton officiated. Katharine was 54 years old and Kay was 65. She had known him for many years. In 1898 her brother had painted a portrait of Dorothy, Kay's daughter by his first marriage to Edith Maude Grahame, so Katharine may have met him then or shortly thereafter. Certainly she knew him in 1900, when he contributed a dedication to the *Album Amicorum* which she kept.[6] By 1909 it seems that they were on intimate terms.[7] What D. Y. Cameron thought of this is not recorded. He was very much the dominant figure in

PLATE 92
Katharine Cameron at her
printing press 1931
National Library of Scotland

PLATE 93
Arthur Kay

the Cameron family and the women were rather in awe of him.[8] Probably he took a rather dim view of the affair.

Arthur Kay was born in London in 1861. His father was a director of Arthur & Co. Ltd., the major Glasgow wholesale warehousing firm, which manufactured and sold textiles throughout Britain and exported them to America and the British Colonies. Prior to the First World War the company was known throughout the British Empire as 'the universal provider'.[9] Kay joined his father on the board in 1887. He had married his first wife in 1886, but it had not worked out. When they separated is not known, but they were divorced shortly before his marriage to Katharine.

He was a very cultured man with a wide range of interests from the business of the company and municipal finance to art and books. Educated at Rossall School in Lancashire and Glasgow University, he had travelled widely before joining the company. He was a true connoisseur and an instinctive and discriminating collector, devoting almost the whole of his leisure time for almost 60 years to art. Like D. Y. Cameron, he could say 'I am a lover of the beautiful who early sought to gather fine things. The taste has clung to me'.[10] It was in his teens that his interest in art was kindled – he bought his first painting (for his father) when he was fifteen years old. On his travels abroad he seized every opportunity to visit museums and galleries, laying the foundation of his vast knowledge of the fine and decorative arts. He became an acknowledged expert in seventeenth century Dutch painting. However, he did not restrict himself to the Old Masters; his interests included the French Impressionists and twentieth century British artists – he collected paintings by William Nicholson, S. J. Peploe and D. Y. Cameron himself. With such an extensive knowledge of art, Kay was often consulted by dealers and collectors; Katharine's nephew Robert later wrote: 'To watch him handle a glass or a bronze was an educational experience, as it was to observe him scrutinising the picture which was of immediate concern, often in the middle of a meal, for you only got to know a picture by living with it, and there would be one on an easel in the middle of their dining-room.'[11] For many years he was closely associated with the Scottish Modern Arts Association, which sought to establish a representative collection of twentieth century Scottish art. His services to art were recognised in 1928 when the RSA made him an Honorary Academician.

Kay was a collector of renown; 'what attracted him was the excitement of the chase, rather than the contemplation of the spoils – there was always something new, something better to be found'.[12] He was one of the first in Britain to recognise the true worth of the Impressionists. In the 1890s he purchased Degas' 'Au Cafe' (now in the Louvre titled 'L'Absinthe') and 'Danseuses avec Contrebasses' (now in New York's Metropolitan Mus-

PLATE 95
Springtime
Watercolour
Peter Haworth

eum), as well as Manet's 'Cafe Place du Theatre Francais' (which Kay sold to William Burrell). Some idea of his catholic taste in collecting can be discerned from what he sold at auction over the years. Old Master paintings and drawings at a two-day sale at Christie's in 1911, no fewer than 1,393 lots of Japanese lacquer-ware in Paris in 1913, part of his extensive library and 60 drawings by Gainsborough at a four-day sale at Sotheby's in 1930 and, following his death, the remainder of his collections, including 106 caricature drawings by Tiepolo, in a two-day sale at Christie's in 1943. Kay had often remarked that he would like to be at the final sale to see the prices realised.[13] However, in the event he would have been disappointed; 1943 was not the best time to sell, but other considerations prevailed. During his lifetime he gifted a number of his paintings to galleries in Britain and Holland.

The Kays' home at 11 Regent Terrace was dedicated to art in its broadest sense. Like Dun Eaglais, it was a veritable treasure house. The Kays' hospitality was both enjoyable and stimulating, in spite of Katharine substituting her favourite beverage of tea for the excellent port which Kay had previously dispensed.[14] They had a wide circle of friends and corresponded with many more. They both knew most of the art community in Scotland and many in England, particularly in London – painters, dealers, curators, collectors. From the theatre Sir John Martin-Harvey, the actor, producer and theatre manager, and his wife Nell were long-standing friends of Katharine and were frequent visitors to both Dun Eaglais and Regent Terrace, when they were on tour in Scotland.

Kay retired from business in 1930, which enabled him to devote even more of his time to the study of art. Katharine and he went on sketching

PLATE 96
Achnacree Moss and Ben
Cruachan *1920*
Watercolour, 10¼ × 15¾
Private Collection

trips to the Highlands. She was particularly fond of the West Highlands around Connel; over many years she spent happy holidays there, painting in the surrounding area – Achnacree Moss, Barcaldine, Benderloch, Dunstaffnage, Kilchurn, Loch Etive. Ben Cruachan was a favourite subject (pl.96). Kay also wrote his memoirs, 'Treasure Trove in Art', which was published posthumously by Oliver & Boyd in 1939; the cover and dust jacket was designed by Katharine. The book is not an autobiography as such, but a series of fascinating stories, describing the excitements and discoveries in a lifetime of collecting.

In December 1928 Katharine had an exhibition of her etchings – 54 in total – at Aitken Dott's Castle Street gallery in Edinburgh. About a quarter of the etchings were no longer available, the editions being exhausted, but the remainder, flower studies and landscapes, which included eight new ones, were for sale priced from one and a half guineas to five guineas. The following year *Haunting Edinburgh* by Flora Grierson was published by John Lanc. In addition to an original etching of Edinburgh Castle by Katharine, the book contained sixteen coloured illustrations and six pencil drawings by her of buildings and scenes in Edinburgh. She was to remark later 'I have had many interesting experiences … especially when making the drawings for *Haunting Edinburgh*, among the wynds and closes of that windswept and romantic city'.[15] It had been almost fifteen years since she had illustrated her last book. Many of the illustrations demonstrate her excellent draughtsmanship; she had some of the same flair for depicting architecture as her brother. However, the colours of some of the plates – particularly the deep blue of the sky – are rather too bright for grey 'Auld Reekie'.

On 21st May 1930 'Boanarges, the Son of Thunder', otherwise known as Iain, was born. This West Highland Terrier later provided an autobiography, interpreted and illustrated by Katharine. *Iain, the Happy Puppy*, published by Moray Press in 1934, was the last book illustrated by her. Her great-nephew Donald Cameron Watt recalls that the dog lived well into old age and was rather unwelcome at Dun Eaglais owing to its incontinence. Katharine would rush around, mopping up after the dog, before D. Y. Cameron should see it![16]

Arthur Kay died on New Year's Day 1939 at the age of 77. Although Katharine and he had spent only ten years as husband and wife, they had known each other for many years before that. They were devoted to each other and those years together had been exceedingly happy. It was truly a marriage of heart and mind in the pursuit of beauty and art.

Katharine was then almost 65 years of age. The house at 11 Regent Terrace was too big for her and in 1940 or the following year she moved to a smaller house at 42 Ormidale Terrace in the Murrayfield district of Edinburgh. Besides, she had to be careful with her money. Her husband's will had been challenged by the family of his daughter by his first wife.[17] Although a settlement was reached, Katharine was left comfortably off, rather than well off.

Katharine continued with her painting, now predominantly flowers. She produced few landscapes after her husband's death, because there was no one to drive her to her beloved West Highlands. She was then still at the

PLATE 97
Columbine with Bees
Watercolour, 17¾ × 5½
Rachel Moss

height of her powers. Reviewing on BBC radio an exhibition of 55 of her watercolours of flowers at the Scottish Gallery in Edinburgh in 1948, the painter and critic R. H. Westwater said:

> 'It is most interesting to notice how superlative quality of this kind can defeat any suspicion of monotony, even when scale and subject matter are so similar throughout … Miss Cameron gives us not only the delicious texture of flower and leaf, the sense of delicate growth and movement expressed with an impeccably sensitive draughtsmanship. She also fills each painting with a pervasive light, a light other than that which actually illuminates her flowers.'[18]

Not only are her watercolours of flowers and plants of 'superlative quality' as paintings, they are also very accurate from a botanical viewpoint. In 1923 she executed a watercolour of a mountain fern unfolding, which is now in the Tate Gallery. The botanist who named this species of fern wrote to the Tate:

> 'The painting is excellent, not only for botanical accuracy – the width and density of the stipe and thachis scales and their darker colour, the absolutely natural arrangement and backward curving of the young fronds … It is also superbly life-like in a way that I have not seen before in fern illustration.'[19]

Katharine allied acute observation to a sensitive painterly technique.

PLATE 98
Roses *1914*
Watercolour over pencil, 16½ × 21¾
Private Collection

Over the next ten years or so she carried on with barely diminished vigour. 'Katharine Cameron has never yielded to the idea that an artist must one day retire from work' wrote Tom Honeyman in 1959.[20] She had moved in 1949 to 8 Henderland Road, a large semi-detached house with a fine view towards the Pentlands and with Mermaid roses climbing up the front – the roses were duly committed to paper and exhibited at the RGI in 1950. The same year she was elected a Fellow of the Royal Society of Arts.

Katharine is remembered as a kind, charming lady, who was very supportive of young artists. She was a mixture of generosity and the reverse – one of her great-nephews recalls getting a present from her of several paper clips from her late husband's desk![21] Small and by then rather stout, she always wore distinctive clothes, usually pale blue or green dresses and flowing scarves – she hated black.[22] She had a wide circle of friends and loved giving tea-parties, 'her table loaded with carbohydrates; later one might get a glass of Crabbie's Ginger Wine, and at 9pm or thereabouts in came her favourite beverage, tea, with scones or cakes'.[23]

Her final one-woman exhibition was held in Glasgow in 1959 at the Sauchiehall Street gallery of T. & R. Annan & Sons. It was also Annan's last exhibition in that gallery before moving to West Campbell Street after an unbroken period of 86 years in Sauchiehall Street. Katharine's show consisted of 56 watercolours and drawings of the West Highlands and Islands done on holidays over many years, which had been treasured by her late husband. Tom Honeyman wrote 'Katharine Cameron is, in her own personal and charming style, as effective with the landscape of Scotland as she is with the flowers of Scotland'.[24] Like Nature in that part of Scotland, Katharine was lavish in her use of colour. She had the same love of the Highlands as her brother and like him she strove to capture in watercolour their magical beauty, their changing moods and light. The exhibition was a great success with over half of the work being sold within a comparatively short time.

At 85 Katharine was beginning to feel her age. Although her mind was remarkably lively virtually to the end, she was suffering more and more from arthritis, walking only with difficulty. Her eyes too were affected by cataracts – 'it's very misty today' she would say on a bright sunny day – and it required considerable persuasion before she agreed to operations, which to her delight were successful.[25] However, she continued with her painting. She was looked after by her old housekeeper Mary. 'Mootey' her cleaner helped her in the studio. In June 1965 Katharine went to stay at her club for a few days, while Mary was on holiday, before going on to Bridge of Allan in connection with her brother's centenary celebrations. At her club she had a fall, which did not seem serious at the time. However, there was a slow deterioration in her condition during July and in early August she had to go into a nursing home. She died on 21st August at the age of 91.

1965 turned out to be a sad year for Scottish art. It had lost two of its foremost women artists – Anne Redpath in January and Katharine Cameron in August. Katharine was the last of 'The Immortals'. Her death also severed one of the few remaining links with Fra Newbery and Glasgow School of Art during that exciting period before 1900, which witnessed the

PLATE 99
Bees and Tropaeolum Speciosa
Watercolour, 8 × 8
Private Collection

birth of the Glasgow Style. She was also the last of the Camerons, a family rich in its artistic abilities in both painting and music.

She achieved recognition and acknowledgement by her own abilities and efforts, not as the sister of Sir D. Y. Cameron. Her command of the medium of watercolour was supreme. She is one of the finest painters of flowers that Scotland has produced. She was a prolific artist and an assiduous exhibitor of her work right to the last. Not a year went by without her submitting work to one or other of the exhibiting societies and usually to two or three. Over the years she also had at least nineteen one-woman shows, including six at Aitken Dott's gallery in Edinburgh and two in America at Boston and Washington. She must have been very disappointed that she was never elected to the RSA, but it must be remembered that in those days it was difficult enough for a woman to be elected, let alone one who specialised in painting flowers in watercolour, however exquisite. Her watercolours continue to be highly regarded more than a quarter of a century after her death.

[1] John Russell Taylor, *The Art Nouveau Book in Britain*, London, 1966, p.138

[2] It has proved impossible to be precise about the number of etchings executed by Katharine Cameron – see Appendix III.

[3] T. J. Honeyman, Katharine Cameron, *Scottish Field*, October 1959, p.27

[4] Ibid., p.27

[5] Rev. Robert James Gordon Watt

[6] NLS ACC8950.19

[7] Watt

[8] Donald Cameron Watt

[9] *Dictionary of Scottish Business Biography*, Vol.2, Aberdeen, 1990, p.331

[10] Colin Clark, Arthur Kay, *Scottish Art Review*, Vol.XIII, No.1, 1971, p.28

[11] Watt

[12] Clark, op.cit., p.28

[13] Watt

[14] Ibid.

[15] Ibid.

[16] Donald Cameron Watt

[17] Watt

[18] R. H. Westwater, 'Arts Review', BBC radio, 19th May 1948

[19] Letter from C. R. Fraser-Jenkins to Tate Gallery dated 4th March 1987 (Tate Gallery Archive)

[20] Honeyman, op.cit., p.28

[21] Donald Cameron Watt

[22] Rev. Robert James Gordon Watt

[23] Watt

[24] Honeyman, op.cit., p.26

[25] Watt

BRIEF CHRONOLOGIES

D. Y. CAMERON

1865	born 28th June in Glasgow
1874-81	educated at Glasgow Academy
1880-84	attended classes at Glasgow School of Art
1881-84	clerk in Glasgow iron foundry and then Perth law office
1884-87	studied art in Edinburgh
1886	exhibited for first time at RSA and RGI
1887	introduced to etching by George Stevenson
	'Paisley Set' published
1889	elected Associate of RE
	'Clyde Set' published by George Stevenson
1891	elected to Glasgow Art Club
	first one-man exhibition at Van Baerle, Glasgow
1892	visited Holland with James Craig Annan
	'North Holland Set' exhibited at Annan, Glasgow
1893	awarded Bronze Medal for etching in Chicago
1894	visited northern Italy with James Craig Annan
1895	first exhibition in America at Fred. Keppel, New York
	elected Fellow of RE
1896	married Jeanie Ure Maclaurin
	honeymoon in Rouen and Dieppe
	exhibition of 'North Italian Set' at Gutekunst, London
1897	joint exhibition with Katharine at Gutekunst, London
	exhibition of etchings at Dotts' Gallery, Edinburgh
	awarded medals for etching in Brussels and Dresden
1898	exhibition of etchings at Connells, Glasgow
	moved to London
	exhibited for first time at IS
	exhibition of etchings in Dundee and Aberdeen
1899	exhibition at Colnaghi, London
	returned to Scotland to live at Kippen
1900	visited Florence, Siena and Venice
	exhibition of etchings at Frost & Reed, Bristol
	'London Set' exhibited at Gutekunst, London
	awarded Gold Medal for etching in Paris
1901	elected member of IS
1902	elected member of SOP
	visited north-west France
1903	resigned from RE along with William Strang
	visited Normandy, Paris and Cluny
	exhibited for first time at RA
1904	elected Associate of RSA and RWS
	'Paris Set' published by A. Strolin in Paris
	formation and first exhibition of Society of Twelve
1905	awarded Gold Medal for etching in Munich
	visited Belgium
1906	elected RSW
1907	exhibition of 'Belgian Set' at Connells, London
1908	exhibition of etchings held by Grolier Club, New York
1908-09	wintered in Egypt
1910	exhibition of etchings at Connells, Glasgow
	possibly visited Paris and northern France
1911	elected Associate-Engraver of RA
	received HON.LLD from Glasgow University
1912	exhibition of etchings at Arthur H. Hahlo, New York
1913	exhibition of etchings at Frost & Reid, London
	exhibition of etchings at Connells, London
1915	elected RWS
1916	elected Associate-Painter of RA
1917-19	war artist for Canadian War Memorials Fund
1918	elected RSA
	appointed to RSA's Scottish War Memorials Advisory Sub-committee
1918-22	no etchings executed
1919	declined nomination for Presidency of RSA
	exhibition of etchings in Pittsburgh, USA
1919-29	member, Faculty of Engraving, British School at Rome
1919-45	member, Faculty of Painting, British School at Rome
1920	elected RA, purchased London house
	exhibition at Aitken Dott, Edinburgh
1920-27	Trustee of Tate Gallery
1920-32	placed on Non-Resident List by RSA
1920-45	Trustee of National Galleries of Scotland
1921	suffered serious heart attack
1922	convalescing in south of France
1923	visited Rome
	received HON.LLD from Manchester University

1924   second visit to Rome

knighted

member of Royal Fine Arts Commission

1925-27   Master Painter for decoration of St. Stephen's Hall

1926   visited south of France

1927-28   extended winter visit to Rome and Naples

1927-38   supervised paintings for rebuilt Bank of England

1928   received HON.LLD from Cambridge University

declined nomination for Presidency of RA

1929   exhibition of watercolours at Cotswold Gallery, London

1931   death of Lady Cameron

1932   reinstated as full member of RSA

1933   member of Royal Fine Art Commission for Scotland

declined nomination for Presidency of RSA for second time

placed on RSA's Retired Academician List

appointed the King's Painter and Limner in Scotland

1934-45   vice-convenor of Church of Scotland's Advisory Committee on Artistic Questions

1936   received HON.LLD from St Andrew's University

1945   died 16th September in Perth

KATHARINE CAMERON

1874   born 26th February in Glasgow

1889-1901   attended classes at Glasgow School of Art

1891   exhibited for first time at RGI

c.1893   elected to Glasgow Society of Lady Artists

1897   elected RSW

joint exhibition with her brother at Gutekunst, London

1898   possibly visited Italy

1900   moved with mother and two sisters to Stirling

first one-woman exhibition at Connells, Glasgow

1902   studied at Academie Colarossi in Paris

1902-14   worked as illustrator of children's books

1908   moved with mother and two sisters to Edinburgh

1909   elected member of SSA

1911   set of 8 flower etchings published by Annan, Glasgow

1913   exhibition at Aitken Dott, Edinburgh

1914   exhibition at Connells, London

1920   elected Associate of RE

1923   exhibition at Connells

1925   exhibition of etchings at Goodspeed's, Boston, USA

1926   exhibition at Fine Art Society, London

1928   married Arthur Kay

exhibition of etchings at Aitken Dott, Edinburgh

exhibition at Wishart Brown, Glasgow

1930   exhibition at Annan, Glasgow

exhibition at Walker's Gallery, London

1931   elected Hon. Member of Glasgow Society of Lady Artists

1932   exhibition at Walker's Gallery, London

1934   exhibition at Parsons' Galleries, Edinburgh

1936   exhibition at Barbizon House, London

c.1938   gave up etching

1939   death of her husband

c.1940   moved to 42 Ormidale Terrace in Edinburgh

1942   exhibition at Aitken Dott, Edinburgh

1944   exhibition at Aitken Dott, Edinburgh

1948   exhibition at Scottish Gallery, Edinburgh

1949   moved to 8 Henderland Road in Edinburgh

1950   elected FRSA

1956   exhibition at Scottish Gallery, Edinburgh

1959   exhibition at Annan, Glasgow

1964   elected Fellow of RE

1965   died 21st August in Edinburgh

SELECTED BIBLIOGRAPHY

SCOTLAND AND GLASGOW

Begg, Rev. R. W. A., *The Renovation of Kippen Parish Church* 1986

Berry, Simon and Hamish Whyte (editors), *Glasgow Observed*, Edinburgh, 1987

Checkland, Sydney and Olive, *Industry and Ethos: Scotland 1832-1914*, The New History of Scotland, Edinburgh, 1984

Drummond, A. L. and J. Bulloch, *The Church in Victorian Scotland 1843-74*, Edinburgh, 1975

Drummond, A. L. and J. Bulloch, *The Church in Late Victorian Scotland 1874-1900*, Edinburgh, 1978

Gibb, Andrew, *Glasgow: the Making of a City*, London, 1983

The Glasgow Academy 1846-1946, Glasgow, 1946

Mozley, Anita Ventura, *Thomas Annan: Photographs of the Old Closes and Streets of Glasgow 1868-1877*, New York, 1977

Smout, T. C., *A Century of the Scottish People: 1830-1950*, London, 1986

Smout, T. C. and Sydney Wood, *Scottish Voices: 1745-1960*, London, 1990

Stewart, John, *The Camerons: a History of Clan Cameron*, 1974

Wiseman, T. P., *A Short History of the British School at Rome*, London, 1990

SCOTTISH ART

Billcliffe, Roger, *The Glasgow Boys: The Glasgow School of Painting 1875-1895*, London, 1985

Billcliffe, Roger (editor), *The Royal Glasgow Institute of the Fine Arts 1861-1989: Dictionary of Exhibitors*, 4 vols, Glasgow, 1990-92

Bird, Elizabeth, *International Glasgow*, Connoisseur, August, 1973

Burkhauser, Jude (editor), *'Glasgow Girls': Women in Art and Design 1880-1920*, Edinburgh, 1990

Dewar, De Courcy Lewthwaite, *History of The Glasgow Society of Lady Artists' Club*, Glasgow, 1950

Gordon, Esme, *The Royal Scottish Academy 1826 1976*, Edinburgh, 1976

Graves, Algernon, *The Royal Academy of Arts: Dictionary of Contributors 1769-1904*, 4 vols, reprint, Calne, 1989

Guichard, K. M., *British Etchers 1850-1940*, London, 1977

Hardie, Martin, *Water-Colour Painting in Britain: III The Victorian Period*, London, 1968

Hardie, William, *Scottish Painting: 1837 to the Present*, London 1990

Holland, Clive, *Student Life in the Quartier Latin, Paris*, The Studio, vol.27, 1902

Howarth, Thomas, *Charles Rennie Mackintosh and the Modern Movement*, London, 1977

Hutchison, Sidney C., *History of the Royal Academy*, London, 1986

Irwin, David and Francina, *Scottish Painters at Home and Abroad*, London, 1975

Martin, David, *The Glasgow School of Painting*, London, 1897

Paperriere, Charles Baile de, *The Royal Scottish Academy Exhibitors 1826-1990*, 4 vols, Calne, 1991

Macmillan, Duncan, *Scottish Art: 1460-1990*, Edinburgh, 1990

National Galleries of Scotland, *The National Collection of Scottish Art*, Edinburgh, 1990

Newbolt, Sir Francis, *History of the Royal Society of Painter-Etchers & Engravers*, Print Collectors' Club, London, 1930

Pickvance, Ronald, *A Man of Influence: Alex Reid*, Scottish Arts Council exhibition catalogue, Glasgow, 1967

Power, William, *Glasgow and the 'Glasgow School'*, Scottish Art Review, vol.1, no.1, Glasgow, 1946

Royal Academy Exhibitors 1905-1970, 4 vols, London, 1985

Scottish Arts Council, *The Glasgow Boys*, exhibition catalogue in two parts, Edinburgh, 1968 and 1971

Spalding, Frances, *British Art Since 1900*, London, 1986

Tanner, Ailsa, *West of Scotland Women Artists*, Helensburgh and District Art Club exhibition catalogue, 1976

Tanner, Ailsa, *Glasgow Society of Lady Artists*, Centenary Exhibition catalogue, Glasgow, 1982

Taylor, John Russell, *The Art Nouveau Book in Britain*, London, 1966

Tippett, Maria, *Art at the Service of War: Canada, Art and the Great War*, Toronto, 1984

D. Y. CAMERON

Auld, Alasdair A, *Sir D. Y. Cameron*, Scottish Arts Council Centenary Exhibition catalogue, Glasgow, 1965

Bayes, Walter, *Paintings & Etchings of D. Y. Cameron*, The Studio, vol.36, 1905

Buchanan, William, *J. Craig Annan and D. Y. Cameron in North Holland*, paper no.20 in *British Photography in the Nineteenth Century* edited by Mike Weaver

Buchanan, William, *The 'most versatile and artistic' James Craig Annan*, The Photographic Collector, vol.5 no.1

Caw, Sir James L., *Sir D. Y. Cameron*, Old Watercolour
    Society, vol.27, 1949

D. Y. Cameron's 'Craigievar', The Art Journal, 1909

Etchings of D. Y. Cameron, The Studio, vol.5, 1895

Finberg, A. J., *Paintings of D. Y. Cameron*, The Studio, 1919

Hind, A. M., *Etchings of D. Y. Cameron*, London, 1924

Meldrum, D. S., *Watercolours of Highlands by D. Y. Cameron*,
    Apollo, October 1929

National Gallery of Scotland, *Prints of D. Y. Cameron and
    William Strang*, exhibition leaflet, Edinburgh, 1986

Rinder, Frank, *D. Y. Cameron: Illustrated Catalogue of His
    Etchings and Drypoints 1887-1932*, Glasgow, 1932

Rutter, Frank, *Recent Etchings of D. Y. Cameron*, The Studio,
    vol.44, 1908

Salaman, Malcolm C., *D. Y. Cameron* , Modern Masters of
    Etching, vols. 7 and 33, 1925 and 1932

Smith, Bill, *David Young Cameron*, Fine Art Society
    exhibition catalogue, Edinburgh, 1990

Stodart Walker, A., *Paintings of D. Y. Cameron*, The Studio,
    vol.55, 1912

Wedmore, Frederick, *Etchings of D. Y. Cameron*, The Art
    Journal, 1901

Wedmore, Frederick, *Cameron's Etchings: a Study &
    a Catalogue*, London, 1903

Wright, Harold J. L., *Etchings & Drypoints of D. Y. Cameron*,
    Print Collectors' Club, London, 1947

KATHARINE CAMERON

Annand, Louise, *Katharine Cameron*, Glasgow Herald, 6th
    March 1959

Clark, Colin, *Arthur Kay*, Scottish Art Review, vol.XIII,
    no.1, 1971

Hanson, Jenny H., *The Landscapes and Flower Pictures of Miss
    Katharine Cameron, ARE, RSW*, Walker's Monthly, London,
    April 1930

Honeyman, T. J., *Katharine Cameron*, Scottish Field, vol.CVI,
    no.682, October 1959

Katharine Cameron, Scots Pictorial, 18th October 1919

Kay, Arthur, *Treasure Trove in Art*, Edinburgh, 1939

Marillier, H. C., *The Romantic Water-colours of Miss Cameron*,
    The Art Journal, 1901

Wright, Helen, *The Etchings of Katherine Cameron*,
    International Studio, vol.75, New York, 1922

APPENDICES

I WORKS EXHIBITED BY D. Y. CAMERON
All works (including etchings) submitted by Cameron
to the principal exhibiting societies in the United
Kingdom are listed. An attempt has been made to
identify work exhibited on more than one occasion –
subsequent exhibitions are noted below the first
exhibition at which the work was shown. In a number
of instances the medium is not clear from the relevant
catalogue.

II WORKS EXHIBITED AT RSW BY
KATHARINE CAMERON

Katharine Cameron was a conscientious exhibitor
throughout her life. Not infrequently she submitted
the same work to different societies and/or to
subsequent exhibitions until it sold. In addition, many
titles are very similar. Consequently, the author
considers that it would be confusing to list all her
work, as has been done in the case of her brother.
The watercolours she exhibited at the RA, RSA and RGI
are recorded in the relevant directory of exhibitors
(see bibliography). However, the watercolours she
exhibited at the RSW are listed here, because details
are not available elsewhere. She did not show any
work at the RWS.

III LIST OF ETCHINGS AND DRYPOINTS
BY KATHARINE CAMERON

As comprehensive details of D. Y. Cameron's etchings
and drypoints are given in *D. Y. Cameron: Illustrated
Catalogue of His Etchings & Drypoints 1887–1932* by
Frank Rinder (Jackson, Wylie and Company,
Glasgow, 1932), they are not listed here.
No such catalogue exists detailing Katharine
Cameron's etchings. Indeed, it has proved impossible
to be precise about the number of etchings executed
by her. A list has been drawn up by the author, based
on one of her notebooks (NLS ACC8650.12), the
catalogue of the Library of Congress in Washington,
which acquired 36 etchings in the early 1920s, Aitken
Dott's 1928 exhibition catalogue of her etchings, the
list of etchings she exhibited at the RE, Phillips' sale
catalogue dated 15th July 1983 and various other

exhibition catalogues, but it cannot be regarded as
exhaustive. The situation is complicated by a suspicion
that some etchings were exhibited in later years under
different titles. Insufficient information is available to
assess the number of states of each etching.

IV PUBLIC COLLECTIONS WITH
PAINTINGS BY D. Y. CAMERON

This is a list of galleries in the United Kingdom
known to have oil paintings by D. Y. Cameron.
Regrettably many are held in store; consequently, it is
essential to check with the relevant gallery beforehand
as to whether a particular painting is on public view
or in store, the latter invariably requiring an
appointment to view.

ABBREVIATIONS

The following abbreviations are used in the
appendices:

IS	International Society
LIV	Autumn Exhibition, Walker Art Gallery, Liverpool
NEA	New English Art Club
RA	Royal Academy
RE	Royal Society of Painter-Etchers and Engravers
RGI	Royal Glasgow Institute of the Fine Arts
RHA	Royal Hibernian Academy
RSA	Royal Scottish Academy
RSW	Royal Scottish Society of Painters in Water-colours
RWS	Royal Society of Painters in Water-Colours
SOP	Society of Oil Painters
SSA	Society of Scottish Artists
ST	Society of Twelve
AQ	Aquatint
D	Drypoint
DE	Drypoint touched with etching
DW	Drawing
E	Etching
E&D	Etching and drypoint
ED	Etching touched with drypoint
O	Oil
S	Sepia
W	Watercolour or wash drawing

Alternative titles are shown in square brackets
Subsequent showings of the same work are listed
below the title.

Year	Venue	Title	Code
1886	RSA	The Convent Minstrel	?O
	RSA	Early Morning in a Highland Valley	?O
	RGI	Jacobites – A Sketch	DW
1887	RSA	Noonday	O
		RGI 1891	
	RSA	Old Edinburgh	?DW
	RGI	Rev W. T. Henderson	O
1888	RSA	Midsummer	O
1889	RSA	The Borderland: Darkening Down	O
		RGI 1890	
	RSA	Traquair: Early Summer	?W
	RE	Ailsa Craig from Arran	E
	RE	Bowden	E
	RE	Evening	E
	RE	A Perthshire Village	E
	RE	St Mary's Loch	E
1890	RSA	Afterglow	?O
	RGI	Autumn Stillness	?W
	RE	Aberdeen Bay	E
	RE	The Cliffs of Aberdeenshire	E
	RE	The Clyde near Carmyle	E
	RE	Clyde Set of 20 etchings	E
1891	RGI	Shadow and Shine	?W
	RE	Bennan	E
	RE	Tweedside [Berwick]	E
	RE	The Docks, Greenock	E
	RE	Dundee	E
	RE	Jean	E
	RE	Loafers	E
	RE	Old Houses, Greenock	E
	RE	Perth	E
	RE	Sketch at Westminster	E
	RE	The Tay	E
	RE	Thames Warehouses	E
	RE	A Thames Wharf	E
	RE	Tweedmouth	E
	RE	The Village Store	E
1892	RSA	Evening Shadows	?O
	RSA	Forty Winks	?O
	RGI	Morning	O
	RGI	Portrait of a Girl	O
	RE	Across the Sands	E
	RE	Anniesland Pits	E
	RE	Begging	D
1892	RE	Dear Aunt Dorothy	E
	RE	A Fisher Lass	E
	RE	Interior [A Highland Kitchen]	E
	RE	Landscape [Landscape with Trees]	D
	RE	Messages	E
	RE	Old Age	E
	RE	Shopping	E
	RE	Speyside	E & D
	RE	Stirling	E
	RE	Sundown	E
	RE	The Three Barrows	E
	RE	The Unicorn, Stirling	E
	RE	The Veteran	E
	RE	Westport	ED
	RE	The White Horse Close, Edinburgh	ED
	NEA	The Building of the Ship	?O
	LIV	Morning on the Teviot	O
1893	RGI	Anemones	W
	RGI	Portrait – Beatrice	W
	RE	The Arch	E
	RE	A Canal, Amsterdam	E
	RE	The Dolphins	E
	RE	A Dutch Damsel	E
	RE	A Dutch Farm	E
	RE	Dutch Interior	E
	RE	The Flower Market	E
	RE	A Lady of Holland	E
	RE	A Lowland River	D
	RE	Morning	E
	RE	Near Haarlem [A Rembrandt Farm]	E
	RE	Night	E
	RE	Oude Kerk, Amsterdam	E
		RGI 1893	
	RE	The Rokin	E
	RE	Rowallan Castle	E
	RE	St John Street, Stirling [Old Houses, Stirling]	E
	RE	The Steps	E
	RE	Storm, Sundown	E
	RE	Three Vagrants	E
	RE	Van Og's Houtkoperij	E
	RE	Van der Deevilij	E
	RE	The Windmill	E
	SSA	Portrait of a Man	O
	NEA	A Dutch Town	O
		RSA 1894	
	LIV	Anemones	O

1894	RGI	Isabel	O
	RGI	Portrait	O
	RE	Book Plates	E
	RE	A Dutch Village	E
	RE	Father Ambrose	E
	RE	Haarlem	E
	RE	Interior, Perthshire	E
	RE	Lecropt	E
	RE	Rowallan's Towers	E
	RE	The Stairs, Rowallan	E
	RE	Stirling Palace	E
		[The Palace, Stirling Castle]	
1895	RSA	Dutch Etchings	E
	RSA	A French Harbour	O
	RSA	Scottish Etchings	E
	RGI	Fairy Lilian	O
		RSA 1896	
	RGI	Portrait	O
	RE	A Border Tower	E
		IS 1907	
	RE	The Bridge of Sighs	E
		LIV 1916	
	RE	Frontispiece	E
		[North Italian Set: Title Page]	
	RE	Tintoret's House, Venice	E
	RE	A Venetian Convent	E
	RE	A Venetian Fountain	E
1896	RSA	Italian Etchings	E
	RGI	Dorothy	?O
	RGI	The Golden Mirror	O
	RE	Holyrood in 1745	E
		RSA 1896	
	RE	St Mark's, Venice (No.1)	E
	RE	Veronica	E
	SSA	Portrait of a Gentleman	O
1897	RSA	The Reverie	O
	RSA	Miss Kathryn Tod, Lasswade	O
	RGI	Daisy	O
		IS 1898	
	RGI	The Sisters	O
	RE	Bookplates	E
	RE	Dryburgh	E&D
		LIV 1916	
	RE	Interior of Italian Wine Farm	E
	RE	Lowland River	E
	RE	Old Houses, Rouen	E
	RE	The Smithy	ED
		IS 1899 LIV 1922	
	LIV	The Bride	O
		RSA 1898	
	LIV	A Dutch Port	O

1898	RSA	Mrs Thomas Annan	O
	RSA	A French River	O
		LIV 1898	
	IS	Braxfield	O
		LIV 1903	
	IS	Portrait of a Lady	O
	RGI	Gipsy	O
	RGI	Robert Meldrum, Esq	O
		LIV 1899	
	RE	Cour des Bon Enfants, Rouen	E
		IS 1899	
	RE	Dieppe Castle	E
	RE	'Ye Banks and Braes'	ED
	LIV	Miss Dorothy Maude Kay	O
		RGI 1900	
1899	IS	Barges	AQ
	IS	The Gargoyles, Stirling Castle	E
		RE 1899	
	IS	Tower Bridge [?The Tower]	ED
	IS	Waterloo Bridge (No.2)	E
		IS 1907	
	RE	3 Bookplates	E
	RE	The Crucifix	E
	RE	Ledaig	E
	RE	The Palace of the Stuarts	E
		IS 1907 LIV 1916	
	LIV	The Avenue	O
1900	RSA	Carselands	O
	RSA	Kirkhill	O
1901	RSA	Early Spring in Tuscany	O
		SOP 1902	
	RSA	Road in Tuscany	?O
	IS	Spring in London	O
		RGI 1904	
	SOP	St. Mark's Evening	O
	SOP	Stirling	O
		RSA 1903	
	RGI	Saint Mark's, Venice	O
		RGI 1929	
	RE	The Abbazia, Venice	ED
	RE	Boquhapple	E
	RE	Elcho on the Tay	E
	RE	Palace, Joannis Darius	ED
		IS 1907	
	RE	The Rialto, Venice	ED
	RE	Siena	ED
		IS 1907	
	RE	St. Mark's, Venice (No.3)	ED
		RGI 1929	
	LIV	The Transept, St Mark's	W

Year		Title	
1901	LIV	A Venetian Doorway	W
		RGI 1902	
1902	RSA	Faraway	O
	SOP	The Valley	O
	RGI	The Ravine	?W
	RE	Laleham	E&D
	LIV	Canale Antonio, Venice – A Study	W
		RGI 1903	
1903	RA	Palace Doorway, Venice	W
		LIV 1903	
	RSA	Menteith	?O
	SOP	Dark Angers	O
		RSA 1904	
	SOP	A Norman Castle	O
	SOP	St. Gervais	O
	SOP	Spring Blossoms, Touraine	O
	RGI	The Winding Road	O
1904	RA	Harfleur	ED
	RA	Montivilliers	ED
	RSA	A Parisian Courtyard	O
		SOP 1904	
	SOP	The Castle Wynd	O
	ST	The Avenue	DW
	ST	Cambuskenneth	E&D
	ST	Early Spring in Tuscany	DW
	ST	The North Porch, Harfleur	ED
		RSA 1905 LIV 1906	
		LIV 1919 LIV 1922	
	ST	Pont Neuf	E
	ST	Saint Germain l'Auxerrois	ED
		RSA 1905	
	ST	Stirling Castle	DW
	RWS¹	Evening, St Jacques	W
	RWS²	Autumn on the Tay	W
	LIV	Stirling Castle	O
1905	RSA	Glencaple	O
		IS 1906	
	RSA	The Old Gateway	O
	ST	The Avenue	E&D
	ST	In the Ardennes	DW
	ST	Murthly on the Tay	E&D
		LIV 1906	
	ST	Neidpath	DW
	ST	Robert Lee's Workshop	E&D
		LIV 1906 RGI 1919 RGI 1921	
	ST	The Sycamore	E&D
	ST	The Tweed at Coldstream	ED
	ST	The Valley	DW
	ST	The Winding Road	DW
	RWS¹	The Waning Light	W
	RWS²	The Citadel	W
1905	LIV	St. Andrews	O
1906	RSA	A Castle in the Ardennes	O
	RSA	Old Brussels	O
	ST	Autumn Stillness	DW
	ST	Berwick on Tweed	DW
	ST	Berwick-on-Tweed	ED
	ST	Pluscarden	E&D
	ST	The Silver Tweed	DW
	ST	St Merri	E&D
	ST	Still Waters	E&D
	ST	A Yorkshire Valley	DW
	RSW	Robin Hood's Bay	W
		RGI 1923	
	RWS¹	Ben Lomond, Sunset	W
	RWS²	Autumn	W
	RWS²	Evening Mists on the Meuse	W
	RWS²	Laroche	W
	RWS²	Whitby	W
		RSW 1907	
	LIV	The Canongate Tolbooth, Edinburgh	ED
1907	RSA	Early Morning, Whitby	O
	RSA	Morning at Berwick	?
	IS	Bookplates	E
	IS	Newgate	E
		LIV 1916	
	IS	The Workshop	E&D
	RGI	The Eildon Hills	O
	RGI	Marij	W
	RGI	A Venetian Street	W
	RWS¹	The Morning Sun, Whitby	W
	LIV	The Clyde	O
1908	RSA	Criffel	O
		RSW 1944³	
	RSA	South Aisle, Tewkesbury	O
	ST	Criffel	DW
	ST	The Little Devil of Florence	ED
		RSA 1908 LIV 1908 RSA 1926	
	ST	Ponte della Trinita, Florence	E&D
	ST	Yorkshire Uplands	DW
	RWS²	Isles of the West	W
1909	RSA	Craigievar	O
		LIV 1909 RGI 1910	
	RSA	The Marble Quarry, Iona	O
		IS 1910	
	IS	Isles of the Sea	O
		LIV 1909	
	ST	Gateway of the Citadel, Cairo	DW
	ST	The Mokattam Hills, Cairo	DW
	ST	The Old Minaret, Cairo	DW
	ST	Ruined Mosque, Cairo	DW

1909	ST	The Turkish Fort, Cairo	DW
		IS 1912³	
	ST	The Walls of Cairo	DW
		IS 1912³	
	RSW	Luxor	W
	RSW	Old Cairo	W
	RSW	A Pillar of Luxor	W
	RWS¹	Chill Dawn	W
		LIV 1909	
	RWS¹	Evening Mists	W
	RWS¹	Notre Dame de la Couture	W
	RWS²	Luxor – Evening	W
	RWS²	A Mosque in Cairo	W
	LIV	The Fort	DW
	LIV	Iona Cathedral	W
1910	RSA	The Hills of Skye	O
		IS 1911 LIV 1911	
	RSA	Nightfall: Luxor	O
		LIV 1910 IS 1911³	
	RSA	Rameses II	ED
		ST 1910	
	ST	Cairo Quarries	DW
	ST	The Desert	ED
		LIV 1910 LIV 1928	
	ST	An Egyptian Mirror	E
	ST	The Hill Fort	DW
	ST	My Little Lady of Luxor	ED
		LIV 1916	
	ST	The Nith	DW
	ST	Sketch on the Tay	E&D
	ST	Sligachan	DW
	ST	Stirling Castle	DW
	ST	The Turkish Fort	ED
		LIV 1910 LIV 1916	
	RWS¹	Tweedside, Evening	W
	RWS¹	Tweedside, Morning	W
	RWS²	Loch Linnhe	W
	RWS²	Speyside	W
		LIV 1920	
	LIV	Beauvais	E&D
1911	RA	Ben Ledi	E&D
		LIV 1911 LIV 1933 RGI 1937	
	RA	The Wingless Chimera	ED
		RHA 1913	
	RSA	Badenoch	O
		IS 1912	
	RSA	Old Paris	O
	RSA	The Sphinx	?O
	RWS¹	The Shining Spey	W
	RWS²	Arran	W
1912	RA	Arran Peaks	DE
1912	RA	Craigdhu	DW
	RA	A Queen of Chartres	D
	RSA	Cir Mhor	O
	ST	Arran Peaks	DW
	ST	Ben Ledi	DW
	ST	The Boddin	D
	ST	A Cat of Bubastis	ED
		LIV 1916	
	ST	Cir Mhor	DW
	ST	Dinnet Moor	D
		LIV 1916	
	ST	Drumadoon	D
	ST	Dun-Fionn	DW
	ST	Dunvalanree	ED
	ST	Early Morning, Brodick Bay	DW
	ST	Lunan	E&D
	ST	Ralia	D
	ST	Redcastle	DW
	RWS¹	Morning Mists, Arran	W
1913	RA	Aquamanile	E&D
		LIV 1913 LIV 1916 RSA 1926	
	RA	On the Tay	E&D
		LIV 1913 RHA 1913 RSW 1944³	
	RA	A Perthshire River	?
	RSA	The Hill of the Winds	O
		RA 1913	
	IS	Inverlochy	O
	IS	The Mountains of Arran	O
	RSW	Mountain Study	W
	RWS¹	Autumn	W
	RWS¹	Autumn in Menteith	W
	RWS¹	Mountain Tops, Arran	W
	RWS²	Glen Rosa	W
	LIV	April Snows – Ben Ledi	O
1914	RA	Appin Rocks	D
	RA	Ben Ledi: Early Spring	O
	RA	Glenmore	?
	RA	The Valley	DW
	RSA	Stirling Castle	O
	IS	Ben Vorlich, Autumn	O
	RSW	Cairngorms	W
	RWS¹	Argyll	W
	RWS¹	Arran Rocks	W
	RWS¹	Braes O'Doune	W
	LIV	The Valley of the Spey	?
1915	RA	The Ochils [The Frews]	D
	RA	Tewkesbury	E&D
		RGI 1915	
	RSA	In Strathearn	W
		LIV 1915	

Year	Society	Title	Medium
1915	RSA	Nether Lochaber	O
		LIV 1915	
	RSA	Perthshire Landscape	W
		LIV 1915	
	IS	Dunstaffnage	O
	IS	Salachan	O
	IS	St. Andrews, Early Morning	O
	RGI	Eilean Creag	?O
	ST	Ben Ledi in Winter	DW
	ST	The Dark Hill	DW
	ST	Dunmyat	DW
	ST	Dunstaffnage	D
	ST	Glen Tarff	DW
	ST	Hills of Tulloch	E&D
	ST	Kincardine	E&D
		LIV 1919	
	ST	On the Forth	DW
	ST	The Pap of Glencoe	DW
	ST	The Valley [Glencrutten]	D
	RWS¹	Perthshire Hills	W
		LIV 1933	
	RWS²	Balquhidder	W
	RWS²	Inverlochy	W
	RWS²	Spring	W
	RWS²	The Stack	W
	RWS²	Uplands in Menteith	W
		RSW 1916	
	RWS²	Vale of Forth	W
	RWS³	Lorne	W
	RWS³	Seil	W
1916	RA	April	O
	RA	Balquhidder	O
	RA	Ben Vair	?
	RSA	Glen Nevis	?O
	RSA	Urquhart	O
	IS	Cruachan Ben	O
	IS	Loch Nell	O
	RGI	The Watch Tower, Berwick	O
	RWS¹	Autumn in Strathtay	W
	RWS¹	A Lowland Farm	W
	RWS²	Castle Urquhart	W
	RWS²	Morven and Mull	W
	RWS²	Old Houses, Chartres	W
	LIV	Clairne Laroche	?
	LIV	Damme	E&D
	LIV	Dinant	E&D
	LIV	The Gateway of Bruges	ED
	LIV	Haddington	ED
	LIV	The Hotel de Sens	ED
	LIV	Rue des Filles Dieu, Angers	E
	LIV	Valley of the Ardennes	E&D
1916	LIV	Yvon	ED
1917	RA	The Hills of Lorne	O
	RA	Rue du Bourg, Chartres	O
		RSA 1918 RGI 1920	
	RA	Spring in Strathearn	O
		IS 1918	
	RSA	St. Aignan, Chartres	O
	RSA	Ypres	O
1918	RA	Cafe Leroux	O
	RA	The Waters of Lorne	O
	RSA	The Sound of Arisaig	O
	RSA	South Morar	O
	RWS²	Blue Lorne	W
	RWS²	Evening	W
	RWS²	Norham	W
	RWS²	The Sound of Mull	W
1919	RA	April Snows, Ben Vorlich	O
	RA	The Oak Staircase	O
	RA	The Sound of Kerrera	O
		RGI 1919	
	RA³	The Ruins of Ypres	O
	RSA	Bailleul	O
	RSA	The Norman Arch (Diploma Work)	O
	IS	Uplands of Lorne	O
	RSW	Loch Ericht	W
	RSW	Waterloo Bridge	W
	LIV	Inverlochy Castle	DE
	LIV	The Meuse	E&D
	LIV	Notre Dame, Dinant	ED
	LIV	The Palace Doorway	E
1920	RA	Durham (Diploma Work)	O
	RA	The Heart of Sutherland	O
	RGI	Ardtornish	O
		RSA 1923 LIV 1923	
	RGI	The Fisher's Hut	E&D
1921	RA	Autumn in Argyll	O
	RA	Durham	O
	RGI	Moonrise in Lorne	O
1922	RGI	Inverlochy Castle	O
	RWS²	Ben Lomond	W
	RWS²	Chon	W
	RWS²	The Narrows of Loch Ard	W
	LIV	Cove	O
	LIV	Doge's Palace	ED
		LIV 1933	
	LIV	Five Sisters, York Minster	ED
	LIV	The Island of Rhum	O
	LIV	Nithsdale	D
	LIV	Strathearn	D
1923	RA	The Hills of Chon: November	O
	RA	The Three Gables	O

Year	Soc.	Title	Code
1923	RA	The Wandering Tides of Morvern	O
	RSA	Ben Slioch	O
	RSA	La Rue Annette	O
	RGI	In Ancient Rome	O
	LIV	Old Ravenna	O
1924	RGI	In the Heart of Sutherland	O
	RGI	The Temple of Venus, Rome	O
		RSA 1924	
	RWS[1]	Ben Lomond	W
	RWS[2]	Chon	W
1925	RA	The Shadows of Glencoe	O
	RA	Sundown, Kerrera	O
	RSA	Baths of Caracalla II	O
		LIV 1925	
	RGI	The Firth of Lorne – November	O
1926	RA	Autumn Snows, Menteith	O
	RA	Kinloch Aline	O
	RA	The Marble Arches, Coliseum, Rome	O
	RSA	The Baths of Caracalla, Rome	O
	RSA	Ben Lomond	E&D
	RSA	A Garment of War	O
		LIV 1926 RSW 1944[3]	
	RSA	Thermae of Caracalla	E&D
		LIV 1928	
	RGI	Thermae of Caracalla, Rome	O
	RWS[1]	Loch Lomond	W
1927	LIV	Far Feochan	O
1928	RA	Edom o'Gordon	O
	RA	The Holy Isles	O
		RSA 1929 LIV 1929	
1929	RA	Cluanie	W
	RA	The Hills of Tay	?
	RA	The Shadowed Valley	W
	RGI	Broad Street, Stirling	ED
1930	RA	The Everlasting Hills	O
	RA	The Rocks of Skye	W
	RA	The Valley of Dean	W
	RSA	Ostia	O
	RWS[1]	The Hills of Skye	W
	LIV	Autumn in Menteith	O
		LIV 1933	
1931	RA	Culloden Moor	W
	RA	Hills of Perthshire	W
	RWS[1]	Loch Ard	W
1932	RA	Loch Earn	O
1933	RA	A Castle in Skye	O
		LIV 1933	
	RA	The Eagle's Crag	W
		LIV 1933	
	RA	Loch Lubnaig	W
	RA	Saint Clement's	W
1933	RWS[1]	The Campsies	W
	LIV	Bonaive Quarries	W
	LIV	Loch Naver	O
	LIV	Morvern	W
	LIV	St. Mark's No.2	E
1934	RA	Hills of Menteith	W
	RA	The Hills of Ross	W
	RA	Menteith	W
	RA	The Rocks of Durness	W
	RA	The Scottish Borders	W
	RA	Suilven	O
		RGI 1937 RSA 1938	
	RGI	Tarff	D
1935	RA	The Heart of Perthshire	O
	RGI	Springtime in Perthshire	?O
1936	RA	Glen Lyon	S
	RA	Loch Eil	S
	RA	Shiehallion	S
	RA	The Wilds of Assynt	O
		RGI 1937	
	RGI	Morning – Dunure	O
1937	RA	The Eagle's Crags	O
	RGI	Stormy Sunset in Skye	O
	RWS[1]	Loch Sunart	W
1938	RA	Lorne	O
	RA	Ben Mhor	S
		RGI 1939	
	RSA	The Roman Campagna	O
1939	RA	Urquhart	S
1943	RGI	Tarff	?O
1944	RGI	The Eternal Hills	O
	RSW	St. Laumer, Blois	ED

[1]   RWS Spring Exhibition
[2]   RWS Winter Exhibition
[3]   Special Exhibition

Year	No.	Title	Price
1893	29	Geranium	£4.4
	228	Roses	£7
1894	125	Sea Birds	£8.8
	441	Geranium and Marigold	£8.8
1896	312	The Brownie	NFS
	380	Golden Goblins	NFS
1898	131	'Hush! remind not Eros of his wings'	£30
	168	White and Crimson	£12.12
	175	The White Butterfly	£15
	178	Purple Chrysanthemums	£12.12
1898 [1]	61	White and Crimson	NFS
	65	Chrysanthemum	NFS
1900	10	Sketch on the Thames	£15
	139	A Baby	£21
	149	Master Robert Laidlaw (miniature)	NFS
	152	Aileen (miniature)	£6
1901	155	Portrait of a Lady	£20
	189	Ullapool, Loch Broom	£8.8
1902	139	Wild Bees	£6.6
	148	The Fairy Pageant	NFS
1903	37	Day-dreams	£10.10
1904 [2]	268	Wild Bees	£5.5
	277	The Statuette	£8.8
	319	The Water Baby	£36
1905	51	The Twelve Dancing Princesses	£10.10
	70	Standard Roses	£31
	80	The Lady of Shalott	£15.15
1906	134	Dierdre	
		The Swineherd	NFS
		The Four White Swans	
	152	Roses and Carnations	£16.16
	156	Little Red Shoes	NFS
		The Seeds of Love	
1907	111	The Little Swineherd	£25
	151	Rose-red and White Rose	£20
	154	Sketch of Marble Quarry at Iona	£16.16
1908	8	The Western Sea	£10.10
	125	When the Sun Goes Down	£16.16
	127	Playmates	£8.8
1909	224	The Black Poppy	£15.15
	284	A Bowl of Roses	£33
1910	54	Amboise	£20
	74	Black Poppy	£14
	102	Aucassin and Nicolette	£16.16
1911	14	Playmates	
1912	8	Elie	£18.18
1912	34	Primroses	£15.15
1913	56	Dream Roses	£30
	63	Bamburgh Castle: Sunset	£12.12
	71	The Black Mill, Winchelsea	£10.10
	267	Apple Blossom	£18.18
1914 [2]	1	April in the Glen	£25
	11	Halcyon Days	£8.8
	159	The Marshes	£18.18
1916	13	Pale Primroses	£15.15
	33	A Dorset Farmhouse	£21
	50	The Butterfly Bronze	£26.5
1917	224	Thistles	£26.5
	227	June Afterglow	£15.15
	228	Full-blown Roses	£30
1918	26	The West Bay	£20
	69	Roses of Memory	£31.10
	75	Pink Roses	£31.10
1919	35	Sweet Eglantine	£35
	45	A Memory	£35
	204	Sunset and Shower	£12.12
	235	Freshly Gathered Roses	£52.10
1920	8	The Butterfly	£21
	132	The Statuette	£31.10
	150	Roses and Wild Bees	£31.10
1921	21	Madonna Blue	£35
	29	Laburnum	£25
	71	Cruachan Ben	£18.18
	288	A Sheaf of Roses	£60
1922	48	The Statuette	£40
	85	Loch Linnhe	£31.10
	89	The Butterfly Bronze	£31.10
	187	Evening	£31.10
1923	63	Aonach-Mhor	£31.10
	158	Elie	£30
	169	Iris	£10.10
	233	Ripe Plums	£36.15
1924	177	Delphiniums and Iris	£52.10
	183	Entrance to Glencoe	£26.5
	187	Cruachan in Mist	£31.10
	245	Autumn Roses	£42
1925	131	Autumn Roses	£75
	161	Iris	£50
	291	Dunstaffnage Bay – Daybreak	£45
1926	22	Roses	£73.10
	25	Appin Head	£15.15
	198	Entrance to Glencoe	£20
	222	June Roses	£31.10

1927	17	Shellister – Iris of the Isles	£35
	39	Niphetos Rose	£40
	160	Spring	£63
	273	The Powder Blue Bowl	£50
1928	15	Niphetos Rose	£52.10
	88	Isle of Skye	£26.5
	178	Irish Fireflame	£42
	182	Peacock Butterflies	£42
1929	30	Western Seas	£25
	207	Iris	£20
	242	Niphetos Rose	£30
	273	Sunset, Loch Etive	£12.12
1930	260	Flowers of Spring	£45
	274	February Flowers	£40
	301	Loch Tromlee	£35
1931	39	Honeysuckle	£30
	253	Achnacree Moss – Afterglow	£25
	285	Michaelmas Roses	£40
	292	October Snow	£30
1932	70	Anemones	£21
	74	Roses	£21
	252	Roses	£21
	285	Achnacree Moss – Late Autumn	£21
1932 [3]	71	The Old Leeds Jug	£15
	83	A Sussex Cottage	£20
1933	43	Wood Sorrel	£15.15
	52	Loch Etive – October Evening	£12.12
	296	Thistledown	£20
	305	Honeysuckle	£35
1934	42	Midsummer Day	£21
	163	Achnacree Moss – Late Autumn	£18.18
	258	Summer in Lorne	£18.18
	293	Azalea	£18.18
1935	32	Thistle and Butterflies	£21
	38	February	£15.15
	161	Anemones	£18.18
	166	Autumn in Glen Nant	£18.18
1936	12	Souvenir (17/1/1936)	NFS
	19	Land of Lorne	£10.10
	132	Evening Primrose	£25
	136	Passion Flower	£21
1937	32	Entrance to Glencoe	£15.15
	51	Zinnias in Sunlight	£25
	67	Zinnias	£25
	89	Honeysuckle and Wild Bees	£36.15
1938	1	Niphetos Rose	£35
	48	Loch Nell – Midsummer	£10.10
	77	Red Admiral Butterflies	£26.5
	120	Iain	£15.15
1939	215	Honeysuckle	£20
	227	Tropaeolum	£30
1940	116	Meadow Goatsbeard	£20
	120	Thistledown	£25
1941	223	The Burning Heart of the Rose	£18
1942	23	Gateway of Moray House	£6.6
	26	Back of the Old Playhouse, Canongate	£6.6
	143	Chinese Bronzes	£18.18
	242	Thistledown	£10.10
	271	November	£15.15
1943	21	Butterflies at Play	£18.18
	35	Mermaid Rose	£20
	222	Riddell's Court, Lawnmarket	NFS
	330	Honeysuckle	£15.15
	378	Smollett's House and the Old Playhouse	NFS
1944	73	April	£15.15
	261	Midsummer Morning	£21
1945	11	Roses at Martinmas	£30
	25	In Silk Attire	£12.12
	44	Good-bye Summer	£15.15
	62	Honeysuckle	£30
1945 [4]	20	In Silk Attire	£12.12
	130	Roses at Martinmas	£30
	139	Honeysuckle	£30
	193	A Basket of Roses [5]	NFS
	195	Aconites	£10.10
1945 [6]	35	Roses at Martinmas	£25
	72	Honeysuckle	£21
1945 [7]	51	Wild Roses	£26.5
	86	Poppies	£26.5
	123	My Wild Ones	£25
1946	59	Moonlight	£26.5
	101	Leaf-nested Primrose	£15.15
	297	October	£30
	318	Candlemas Day	£15.15
1947	18	Almond Blossom	£31.10
	77	Honeysuckle	£18.18
	120	Late Autumn Rosebuds	£31.10
	148	Carnations	£31.10
1948	153	Birthday Bouquet	£45
1949	42	Midsummer Eve	£40
	45	Goodbye Summer	£40
	309	October Roses	£45
1950	10	Return of Spring	£25
	47	Honeysuckle	£45
	57	Almond Blossom	£31.10
1951	116	The Burning Heart of the Rose	£45
	210	The Blue Bells of Scotland	£25
	220	Late Autumn – Glen Dochart	£25
	226	St Valentine's Day	£25
1952	266	Goodbye Summer	£35

1952	323	Love in the Mist	£16.16
	343	Languishing, Glorying, Glowing, their Life Away	£65
1953	175	Fallen Petals	£55
1954	95	The Burning Heart of the Rose	£50
	315	Roses in a Chinese Jar	£45
1955	16	White Japonica	£14.14
	19	Love-in-the-Mist	£15.15
	91	Crimson Roses	£50
1956	86	Late Autumn – Glen Nant	£35
1957	131	Rosegarden – Summer Evening	£45
	158	Mermaid Rose	£50
	264	Love-in-the-Mist	£18.18
	410	Honeysuckle	£18.18
1958	237	"Consider the Lilies"	£45
	252	Mermaid Rose	£50
	278	Bluebells of Scotland	£18.18
1959	4	Midsummer Eve – Loch Etive	£35
	219	Evening – Connel Ferry	£15
	226	Afterglow – Cruachan Ben	£35
	284	Dawn – Land of Lorne	NFS
1960	44	Cruachan Ben – Afterglow	£40
	219	The Burning Heart of the Rose	£52
	223	White and Purple Irises	£42
	362	Dawn – Land of Lorne	NFS
1961	89	Barcaldine Castle, Benderloch	£20
	125	My Wild Ones	£40
	327	Roses in September	£40
	344	Wild Roses	£35
	348	Rose Mermaid	£40
1962	71	Midsummer Roses	£20
	106	Rose Garden	£42
	148	Benderloch, Argyll	£45
	198	Magnolia Stellata	£15.15
	210	Cruachan Ben – Afterglow – Loch Awe	£20
1963	78	Merry June	£50
	138	Bluebells	£30
	145	Castle Stalker, Port Appin	£20
1963	166	Midsummer Garden	£60
	340	Gooseberry Bush	£25
1964	293	Flowers of June	£30
	310	Roses in Twilight	£42
	346	Magnolia	£35
1965	174	Brambles and Butterflies	£42
	332	Iris of the Isles	£35
	379	Gooseberry Bush	£20

POSTHUMOUSLY [8]

1966	347	Benderloch, Achnacree Moss
	348	Seven Buds
	349	Sunset at Taynuilt, Loch Etive, Argyll
	350	Gathering Storm – Taynuilt
	351	October Roses
	352	A Bouquet of Roses
	353	Snowdrops
	354	The Far Cuillins

[1] RSW exhibition at People's Palace, Glasgow
[2] Joint exhibition with Glasgow Art Club
[3] RSW exhibition on board SS 'Tuscania'
[4] RSW exhibition, Kelvingrove Art Gallery, Glasgow
[5] Diploma Work
[6] RSW exhibition in Perth
[7] RSW exhibition in Aberdeen
[8] Lent by various collectors

No.	Year	Title	Type	Dimensions
1	1898	Wild Bees	E	$8\frac{1}{4} \times 2$
2	1909	April *bees and blackthorn blossom*	E	$9\frac{1}{2} \times 3\frac{1}{2}$
3	1909	The Tryst *bees and blackthorn blossom*	E	$10 \times 6\frac{3}{8}$
4	1910	Bookplate for Arthur Kay	E	?
5	1910	Bookplate for Arthur Kay	E	?
6	1910	Benjamin [1] *hairy caterpillar*	E	$6\frac{1}{2} \times 2$
7	1910	The Outcast [1] *cherub and rose*	E	$11\frac{7}{8} \times 4$
8	1910	Spring [1] *bees and blossom*	E	$11\frac{7}{8} \times 4\frac{1}{2}$
9	1910	Goodbye Summer [1] *Michaelmas Daisy*	E	$11\frac{7}{8} \times 4\frac{3}{8}$
10	1911	Butterflies [1]	E	$5\frac{7}{8} \times 6\frac{1}{8}$
11	1911	The Chase [1]	E	$9\frac{7}{8} \times 4\frac{3}{4}$
12	1911	Thistledown [1]	E	$12\frac{7}{8} \times 4\frac{7}{8}$
13	1911	Honeysuckle [1]	E	$6 \times 5\frac{7}{8}$
14	1911	Larkspur and Bee	E	$11\frac{7}{8} \times 4$
15	1911	Love in the Mist and Wasps	E	$9\frac{1}{4} \times 7\frac{1}{8}$
16	1912	Columbine	E	$12\frac{1}{4} \times 4$
17	1912	Wild Violets	E	$6\frac{7}{8} \times 7\frac{7}{8}$
18	1913	Bookplate for Arthur Kay	E	?
19	1913	Passion Flower [2]	E	$5\frac{7}{8} \times 5\frac{7}{8}$
20	1913	Thistle [2]	E	$7\frac{3}{8} \times 6\frac{3}{8}$
21	1914	The Race [2] *two caterpillars climbing stalks*	E	$12\frac{7}{8} \times 3$
22	1914	Ben Lora [2]	E	$5\frac{1}{2} \times 8\frac{7}{8}$
23	1914	Blackthorn [2]	E	$5 \times 5\frac{7}{8}$
24	1914	Loch Nell [2]	E&D	5×11
25	1914	The Bay [2] *Elie*	E	$4\frac{1}{2} \times 10\frac{1}{2}$
26	1914	Coastal Scene with Bass Rock in the Distance [3] *unfinished*	E&D	3×13
27	1915	Newark Castle and St Monans	E&D	$2\frac{3}{8} \times 4$
28	1915	Grass of Parnassus	E	$14\frac{5}{8} \times 5\frac{1}{2}$
29	1915	The Swan Inn *Midhurst, Sussex*	E&D	$5\frac{7}{8} \times 4\frac{7}{8}$
30	1915	Goatsbeard	E	$14\frac{3}{4} \times 5\frac{1}{4}$
31	1915-1918	Sea Campion and Blue Butterflies	E	$10\frac{7}{8} \times 5$
32	1916	Old Fishing Town – Hastings	E	$4\frac{3}{8} \times 14$
33	1916	Corfe Castle	E&D	$5\frac{1}{2} \times 13$
34	1916	The Moorland Farm	E&D	$4 \times 9\frac{1}{8}$
35	1916	Rose Burnett *bees and wild rose*	E	$5\frac{7}{8} \times 7$
36	1917	Beregonium *Argyll*	E&D	$5\frac{1}{8} \times 8\frac{1}{2}$
37	1917	Lochan-nan-Rath	E&D	$6\frac{1}{8} \times 12\frac{1}{4}$
38	1917	The Monastery *Amberley*	E&D	$5\frac{1}{2} \times 13\frac{3}{8}$
39	1917	Tortoiseshell Butterflies	E	$11\frac{3}{8} \times 4\frac{3}{4}$
40	1917	Bookplate for Robert Shaw Miller	E	?
41	1918	Flitting *snail on twig*	E	$2\frac{5}{8} \times 3\frac{3}{8}$
42	1918	Kirk and Keep	E	$6\frac{1}{8} \times 12\frac{5}{8}$
43	1918	Monsieur Cobweb *cherub, bee and thistle*	E	$8\frac{1}{8} \times 6\frac{7}{8}$
44	1919	Bookplate for Arthur Kay	E	?
45	1919	The Duel	E	$5 \times 5\frac{1}{2}$
46	1920	Rambler Roses and Red Admirals	E	$7\frac{7}{8} \times 6\frac{7}{8}$
47	1920	Plum Blossom	E	$10\frac{1}{2} \times 4\frac{1}{2}$
48	1920	Honeysuckle	E	$10\frac{7}{8} \times 5$
49	1920	Newark [3] [4]	E&D	$4\frac{3}{4} \times 10\frac{7}{8}$
50	1921	Edinburgh Castle	E&D	$6\frac{7}{8} \times 12\frac{1}{4}$
51	1921	Kilconquhar [3]	E	$5 \times 10\frac{1}{2}$
52	1921	Kingdom of Fife [5]	E&D	$3\frac{7}{8} \times 8\frac{7}{8}$
53	1921	Bees	E	$19\frac{1}{8} \times 7$
54	1921	Eriska	E&D	$4\frac{1}{8} \times 7\frac{1}{4}$
55	1922	Love in the Mist	E	$7\frac{1}{2} \times 9$
56	1923	Dragonfly	E	$13\frac{3}{4} \times 4\frac{3}{4}$
57	1923	Grass of Parnassus and Bog Myrtle	E	$4\frac{7}{8} \times 12\frac{7}{8}$
58	1923	Bees over a Mountainous Landscape [3] *unpublished*	E	$7\frac{7}{8} \times 6\frac{3}{4}$
59	1924	Jack-go-to-bed-at-noon	E	$19\frac{1}{4} \times 7\frac{1}{8}$
60	1924	Barcaldine Castle [6]	E&D	$10\frac{7}{8} \times 13\frac{5}{8}$
60a		Barcaldine	E&D	$5\frac{7}{8} \times 10\frac{7}{8}$
61	1926	Cruachan: Twilight	E&D	$5\frac{1}{4} \times 9\frac{1}{4}$
62	1926	Castle Stalker	E&D	$6\frac{7}{8} \times 11$
63	1926	McConnachie *young hedgehog*	E	$5 \times 7\frac{1}{2}$
64	1926	Entrance to Glencoe	E&D	$4 \times 9\frac{1}{8}$
65	1926	Highland Loch Surrounded by Mountains [3]	E&D	?
66	1927	L'Auberge *Bayeux*	E&D	$10\frac{3}{8} \times 7\frac{1}{8}$

67	1927	Morven	E & D	$5\frac{3}{4} \times 10\frac{1}{8}$
68	1928	Iris	E	$12\frac{3}{8} \times 6\frac{3}{8}$
69	1928	Dark Columbine	E	$11\frac{7}{8} \times 5\frac{3}{4}$
70	1928	The Old Bee	E	$5\frac{7}{8} \times 5$
71	1928	The Rivals	E	$12\frac{3}{8} \times 4$
72	1928	The Mountain Fern	E & D	$17 \times 7\frac{1}{2}$
73	1928	Rose and Bee	E	$5\frac{1}{2} \times 5$
74	1931	Kilchurn [7]	E & D	$7\frac{7}{8} \times 12$
75	1931	Amberley [8]	E & D	?
76	1931	A Highland Keep [8]	?	?
77	1933	Passion Flower	E	?
78	1933	Achnacree Moss	E & D	$9\frac{3}{4} \times 13\frac{1}{4}$
79	1933	Butterflies at Play	E	$12\frac{3}{4} \times 6$
80	1933-34	Dunstaffnage	E & D	?
81	1936	Seven Bees	E	$12 \times 4\frac{1}{2}$
82	1936	Columbine and Butterflies	E	$12 \times 4\frac{3}{8}$
83	1937	Goatsbeard and Butterfly	E	?
84	1938	Butterfly	E	?

[1] Annan set 1911

[2] Connell set 1914

[3] Not recorded in Katharine Cameron's notebook of etchings

[4] May be cut-down version of 'Kirk and Keep'

[5] May be cut-down version of 'Kilconquhar'

[6] Plate cut-down at some time

[7] Notebook of etchings indicates the possibility of two versions

[8] Notebook of etchings records plates cut-down and re-etched (no further details)

IV PUBLIC COLLECTIONS WITH PAINTINGS BY D.Y.CAMERON

SCOTLAND

Aberdeen	Art Gallery
Dundee	McManus Galleries
Edinburgh	National Gallery of Scotland
	City Art Centre
Glasgow	Art Gallery and Museum, Kelvingrove
	Hunterian Art Gallery
Greenock	The McLean Museum
Kilmarnock	Dick Institute Museum and Art Gallery
Kirkcaldy	Museum and Art Gallery
Milngavie	Lillie Art Gallery
Paisley	Museum and Art Gallery
Perth	Museum and Art Gallery
Stirling	Smith Art Gallery and Museum

ENGLAND

Birmingham	Museum and Art Gallery
Bradford	Cartwright Hall Art Gallery
Bristol	Museum and Art Gallery
Cambridge	Fitzwilliam Museum
Liverpool	Walker Art Gallery
London	Imperial War Museum
	Tate Gallery
Manchester	City Art Gallery
Newcastle	Laing Art Gallery
Oxford	The Ashmolean Museum
Port Sunlight	Lady Lever Art Gallery
Preston	Harris Museum and Art Gallery
Rochdale	Art Gallery
Southampton	City Art Gallery
Stoke-on-Trent	City Museum and Art Gallery

IRELAND

Dublin	The Hugh Lane Municipal Gallery of Modern Art

INDEX

INDEX OF WORKS MENTIONED IN TEXT

ACKNOWLEDGEMENTS

Permission to reproduce the following plates is gratefully acknowledged:

Aberdeen Art Gallery
pl. 54

T. & R. Annan & Sons Ltd
pls 1. 15

Bourne Fine Art
pl. 12

Bradford City Art Gallery
pl. 48

Clydesdale Bank PLC
pls 5, 19

Dundee City Art Gallery
pl. 65

Edinburgh District Council:
City Art Centre
pl. 63

The Fine Art Society
pl. 58

Robert Fleming Holdings Limited
pls 3, 8, 17, 18, 30, 41, 47, 49, 51, 52, 55, 77, 86

Garton & Co.
pls 9, 29, 33, 38, 40, 57, 61

Glasgow Museums: Art Gallery & Museum, Kelvingrove
pls 4, 13, 27, 46

Imperial War Museum, London
pl. 64

Kirkcaldy Museum & Art Gallery
pls 34, back jacket

Manchester City Art Galleries
pls 22, 26

Duncan R. Miller Fine Arts
pl. 39

Ewan Mundy Fine Art pl. 62

National Gallery of Scotland
pls 7, 35, 50, 69, 76

National Library of Scotland
pls 2, 92

Perth Museum & Art Gallery
pls 75, 84

Harris Art Gallery, Preston
pl. 74

Royal Academy of Arts, London
pl. 68

Royal Scottish Academy pl. 67

Sotheby's
pl. 42